A MAN MANY ADMIRED

MY
FATHER

PARVATHI UPPALURI

Dedication

To my mother,

the personification of patience, who unconditionally supported my father at every step of his journey and sustained our family.

Contents

Contents

FOREWORD

The decision of my sister, Smt. Parvathi Uppaluri, the eldest among us siblings, to write the biography of our father, was warmly welcomed by all of us for more than one reason. She, being the the first born, has memories of our father when he was younger. Her time spent in the village with my grandparents sets the stage most charmingly to narrate our father's early childhood.

Beyond the obvious desire to revisit the life of our illustrious father, the deeper purpose lies in narrating his life journey, which is an inspiring tale of courage, conviction, and dharma. His vision and philosophy resonate as a compelling narrative to be shared with everyone.

For older readers, this biography will evoke a nostalgic journey back into rural India and the interconnectedness of extended families, a society untouched by modernism yet burdened by foreign rule. For younger readers, it offers a fascinating insight into the close bonds of family and community, which is in contrast with their familiarity with modern nuclear family structures. In essence, this biography not only recounts the life of our father but also mirrors the journey of a striving youth's struggle for self-discovery and professional achievement.

The narrative begins with a dramatic incident that compelled my father, then a recent graduate, to embrace the Law as his profession amidst challenging circumstances. His acute understanding of societal dynamics, shaped by the enduring impact of colonial rule, remains remarkable to this day. The author skilfully narrates the chronology of our father's life with a deep understanding of events, gathered meticulously from family, friends and father's colleagues.

She brings out distinctly our father's philosophy of life with many narratives, making one wonder if she witnessed events unfolding right in front of her eyes. This simply shows how intimate and close her understanding of facts and experiences of situations were.

It was Parvathi's determination and perseverance that our father's full life journey, given by a constant desire to lead a just and dharmic life will now be available in a way that will be accessible to all.

I am sure the biography will be an absorbing, illuminating and inspiring read for people of all ages.

Dr. Sri Lakshmi Peddada

Author's Note

This book has emanated from my father's blessings and divine will. The idea of writing his biography never once crossed my mind. I always had a deep-rooted wish that many should know about my father's life. Little did I know about how that wish was to be realised!

On a particular day, as I was preparing working manuals for my school teachers, my mind wandered to memories of my grandparents and their profound love for my father. Almost instinctively, I found myself flipping to a few blank pages in my notebook and scribbling down those recollections. Without conscious effort, my thoughts poured out, and I filled about twenty pages without pause or striking any words. Stopping to catch my breath, I read through what I had written before going further, and felt satisfied and happy with what I wrote.

When I shared this experience with my husband, he encouraged me to keep going, suggesting it was a blessing from my father. When I had to face long periods of time, unable to write due to personal contingencies, I would often doubt my ability to continue, fearing that the flow of inspiration would cease. However, to my surprise, every time I sat down to write, the words flowed effortlessly, defying my doubts.

A committed family man, my father ensured that it was not only his immediate family that felt his unwavering support, but his extended family, and others also who came in contact with him, all felt the same. He pursued knowledge and scholarship fervently, both in his professional endeavours and in his personal pursuits. A compassionate individual, he cared deeply for the well-being of society, the country, and the world at large. His relentless quest for truth and liberation reminds one of none other than King Janaka, the philosopher king.

I wish for those who are familiar with my father to gain deeper insight into his life's journey and the path that shaped him into the person he became. For those who didn't know him, I hope they understand that success is attainable despite adversity, emphasizing the importance of adhering to one's principles in achieving one's goals, whatever they may be.

Acknowledgments

I want to thank:

Dr. Bindu Madhav Uppaluri: My husband, who encouraged me all along and has been there for me through this journey.

Sri Lakshmi: My sister, she patiently listened to my complaints, fears, and doubts, encouraged and supported me in every way, contributed anecdotes from our father's life and been with me all along.

My brothers

P. Sri Raghuram, my brother, readily shared a number of incidents and information not known to me about our father, and encouraged me.

Kasi Viswanath: From the outset my brother encouraged me and said, "You are the one who should write father's biography." He researched and provided information about our family history and our roots.

P.S. Narasimha, my little brother, provided information on my father's professional achievements. He also patiently listened to my saga and gave unconditional support, encouraging me despite his busy schedule.

Raseshwari Chonkar: Dear friend Rasu has done the first edit and extended her valuable advise.

Saraswati: Saraswati reviewed one of the earlier manuscripts and motivated me to work further.

K. S. Viswanatham: our friend, who read the draft from beginning to the end and made technical suggestions.

Lastly, I would not miss thanking my children, Aparna, Srinivas and Sravanti who stood by me and gave me rock-solid support. My eldest daughter Aparna Uppaluri helped in the final edits.

I thank the publishers, especially Joshua, my publishing manager, and Abhinesh Rolla for patiently listening to my queries, providing clarifications, and bringing out this work.

I would like to thank the following eminent personalities who have taken time to write about my father.

Honourable Justice B. P. Jeevan Reddy;

Sri V.R. Reddy, Former Additional Solicitor General of India and Former Advocate General of Andhra Pradesh;

Sri K. Aravinda Rao; Retired Director General of Police, Andhra Pradesh;

Sri Salaka Raghunatha Sarma; Eminent Sanskrit and Telugu Pandit, Recipient of Rashtrapati Puraskar;

Sri Jai Prakash; Senior Advocate, Standing Counsel, Tirumala Tirupati Devasthanam;

Justice Sanjay Kumar; Judge Supreme Court of India;

GLOSSARY

Garu:	Addressing elders with respect in Telugu (e.g., Gandhi Garu, Nehru Garu).
Amma:	Mother
Nanna:	Father
Nayana:	Another form for father, addressing with affection.
Annayya:	Elder brother.
Vadina:	Elder brother's wife.
Akkayya:	Elder sister.
Bava:	Sister's husband.
Attayya:	Paternal aunt.
Mamayya:	Maternal uncle.
Ayya:	Workers address the landlords with respect, especially in villages.
Satram:	A place where travelers lodge.

Chapter 1
BALANCE OF CHOICES

In 1947, the British permanently departed from India, and the entire nation rejoiced in its newfound independence with a great sense of freedom and happiness . The elderly, who never thought they would witness India's liberation, were filled with joy and a profound sense of peace, finally able to experience life in a free India. Meanwhile, the younger generations felt that a world of opportunities was about to unfold for them, free from the constraints of colonial rule.

Young Kodandaramayya had successfully graduated with a commerce degree from Andhra University in Visakhapatnam. Determined to find a job right away, he eagerly plunged into job search, certain to find employment as he was now a university graduate. He thought 'my parents have been working relentlessly to sustain the family. They need to rest now. Both my sisters are sitting in the village without proper education. I need to take care of that and bring my wife home who has been patiently waiting at her parents's house.'

After connecting with a few contacts suggested by his teachers and seniors, he received vague and unhelpful responses, leaving him uncertain about his job prospects. Feeling confused, he decided to travel to Guntur, where he hoped to meet an officer recommended by his teacher, believing this might lead to better opportunities.

Arriving at the officer's residence around 3 PM Kodandaramayya introduced himself to the person who answered the door, mentioning that Mr. Subbarao from Visakhapatnam had sent him to meet the officer. Invited in, he waited nearly twenty minutes until the officer entered the room. Kodandaramayya quickly rose, greeted him respectfully, and presented the letter from his teacher.

The official examined the letter and inquired about Kodandaramayya's college and job preferences. While Kodandaramayya remained standing, the officer instructed him to take a seat and posed additional questions. Kodandaramayya continued standing, answering him respectfully. The official insisted that he sit down. After Kodandaramayya sat down, he continued asking a few more questions and then abruptly dismissed Kodandaramayya, saying that he would write to Subba Rao. Perplexed, Kodandaramayya greeted him and left. He wrote to his teacher who referred him to this officer about the interview.

He came to Vijayawada from Guntur and stayed with his cousin, Dr Gurunatha Rao, and was eagerly awaiting news from his teacher. During this time, he continued his job search but did not get any positive results. He thought, 'Looks like only recommendations work. Let me wait for the response from my teacher's friend.' Two days later, he received the letter. Kodandaramayya was aghast reading it. He went straight to Gurunatha Rao, giving the letter to him said, "Please read," with an agitated look on his face.

Gurunatha Rao read the letter and said, "What is this? What exactly happened there? Please tell me." Kodandaramayya, in his disappointment and unexpected turn of events, said, "That is it. I am going to study Law. Since I went to Visakhapatnam, I very much wanted to study Law, but considering my family's financial situation, I have decided to take up a job. After making sincere efforts to procure employment, the results are disheartening. Now this letter, it has decided everything." Gurunatha Rao looked at him and thought, 'Something serious must have happened.' He said, "Wait, wait, don't get agitated. Let's see," and read the letter once again. He paused for a while and then said, "So you don't want to look for more jobs after this. This is one bad experience. Why lose hope so fast and give up the idea of a job so soon? Not every place or person will be the same. Try a few other places."

Kodandaramayya turned to his cousin and said, "I've been actively seeking employment since I completed my exams, as I was confident that I would certainly pass. Unfortunately, not a single interview call or one positive response has come my way. How long can I be unemployed and sit around doing nothing. I know, few my friends are also going through the same situation. This means we have been having false hopes and the situation is not good. I understand that we just got our independence, it will take a while for the country to settle down, but that does not solve my problem. Instead of sitting around waiting for a job, I can improve my quaifications so that I will be better equipped and have better chances to be employed.

After all the struugles and the sacrifices our leaders made, is this the life we are destined to lead? It's not just the British, even our own people have adopted a similar demeanour after working with them. This behaviour, influenced by the bureaucracy of the British and slave mentality, seems to have seeped into us, thanks to them, I fear it might persist even after our independence. Whether it's the British or our own higher officials, the mistreatment of subordinates seems to prevail. They not only rule us physically, but they go deep in and touch the core of our souls, and the corruption manifests at a profound level."

"Now, I understand why individuals of integrity prefer independent professions over jobs. The legal profession, being one of the most dignified, is evident in the choices of our honourable freedom fighters. Opting for a profession would allow me to earn a respectable income with dignity. I desire the opportunity to showcase my abilities and evolve in various aspects. Only independent professions provide such prospects. Taking up a job, I fear, would confine me within the bureaucratic constraints, where individual efforts and creativity carry little weight. A professional career, on the other hand, presents daily challenges that foster holistic growth. I understand it may seem like I'm focused on my personal aspirations and ideologies, but I believe that, in the grand scheme and over time, my becoming a professional would also prove beneficial for my family, despite the anticipated two more challenging years for all of us."

Gurunatha Rao patiently heard Kodandaramayya's frustration and said, "Kodanda, just tell me what has happened there. Is it not important for me to know? We will do what is best for you and what you want, but let us look at things more objectively." Somehow, this calmed Kodandaramayya. He smiled and narrated the whole scenario of what happened at Guntur. After pausing for a few seconds, Kodandaramayya said, "you have seen what he has written."

Like I said earlier, it is not that I suddenly decided to study Law. I have been thinking about it for a while. I strongly feel that I have to take that path now. It is a matter of two years. Looking at the situation, I don't know how long it will take for me to get a decent job. Once I earn a degree in Law, I don't have to beg anyone for a job. Many more doors will open up. I will have both options, either to take up a job or to pursue legal practice independently. The beauty of this profession is, if I work hard and become a good lawyer, I don't have to depend on anyone."

Looking at the letter in Gurunadha Rao's hand, he further added, "He says that I lack manners so he cannot consider me for any job. That is because I sat down when he asked me to sit. He expects that, in spite of him asking me to sit down, I should not sit but say 'it's all right, Sir" and continue standing. See, what he says in the letter. 'when I asked him to sit, he simply sat down, looks like he has no manners, so I cannot consider him for any position.' This is the result of the foreign rule. This kind of mentality has seeped into our minds, and this will continue.

Gurunatha Rao nodded his head. He then said, "Kodandaramayya, all that you say is correct. I don't disagree; everything you said is very true. Now, when we consider our personal circumstances, is it not important that you take up a job and start earning? The entire family is hoping that you will do so. How long do you think your father can support you? We all know that his income has reduced significantly. The family has to sustain itself. How long can your wife sit in her parent's house? What about your sisters? Parents are not getting younger, especially your father. Have you considered all this?" He looked at Kodandaramayya inquiringly and added, "Kodanda, I understand your perspective, and your reasoning makes sense. But remember, the path you choose should also consider the practical needs of your family. We're not living in ideal circumstances, and sometimes we have to make compromises for the sake of our loved ones."

Kodandaramayya let out a sigh and took a few minutes before answering. "Do you think that I have not considered any of this? It is not an emotional decision that I have taken, just because I am upset with this one incident. It is not that my ego is hurt, and I am doing this to prove something to someone. In a profession, I will be able to earn a decent amount with dignity. I would like to have an opportunity to prove myself and grow in every way. Only independent professions have that kind of opportunity. In a job, I will be stuck in the bureaucracy. There, my efforts or my creativity will not matter much. In a profession, every day is a challenge, and I will grow in a multi-faceted way. You may be feeling that I am only thinking about myself, my passion and my ideologies. I know my family will be put through two more years of tough time. In a bigger picture, and in the long run, is it not beneficial for my family also if I become a professional?"

As they were talking, Satyanarayana, the elder brother of Gurunatha Rao, walked in carrying bags of vegetables, fruits, and a couple of bags with some grains. Seeing this, Gurunatha Rao and Kodandaramayya hurried toward him and quickly took all the bags from his hands. Gurunatha Rao said, "Annayya, you never listen to me. How many times did I tell you not to carry and bring all that you brought? Why do you carry all these? There is no direct bus from our village. Changing buses and carrying all these, I can't bear to see you doing this."

One could feel his frustration, helplessness, and at the same time, affection for his elder brother in his voice. Kodandaramayya quietly put all the things down and went quickly into the kitchen to fetch a glass of water. He too treated Satyanarayana as his elder brother and respected him.

After drinking the water that Kodandaramayya gave him, Satyanarayana said, "Subbayamma (their widowed sister living in Vijayawada with her 2 young sons) and you always have a flow of relatives. People from our village come for court work, treatment, or various other kinds of tasks. Any amount of food is not enough. Subbayamma is cooking round-the-clock for these people and entertaining them. Sometimes she feels embarrassed to tell you when supplies run out."

Saying this, he went to wash up. Gurunatha Rao looked at Kodandaramayya and said, "Look, Annayya is here. He knows the ways of the world better than anyone. He will surely understand and give us sound advice. He is wiser than anyone I know."

Kodandaramayya nodded his head and fell into his own thoughts. When Satyanarayana walked in, looking at Kodandaramayya said, "Kodanda, very happy that you have graduated. Did you start looking for a job?" Gurunatha Rao quietly narrated the whole scenario of what had happened and the decision Kodandaramayya was about to take, in few words. Satyanarayana kept silent for a while. Then looking at Kodanda, he said, "It is fine, Nayana. There is not much to think about it. Yes, it will be tough for the family and you. If you want to study further, we will figure it out. No one in our families has gone for higher studies like this. Now don't think too much of it. Did you discuss with your parents and did you tell your wife?"

Kodandaramayya nodded his head, saying, "I will be going to Ganapavaram now and discuss with my parents. After taking their consent, I will go to Kalavakur and talk to Satyam."

Gurunatha Rao said, "Now relax. Annaya gave his consent; all will be ok now. We will go and have lunch with Akkayya and tell her. She will be happy too. You can take her blessings also. Tomorrow, you can go to Ganapavaram by the first bus."

Satyanarayana, looking at Kodandaramayya, said, "Should I also accompany you? It has been a while since I saw Annayya." Kodandaramayya immediately said, "Annayya, not now. Let me talk to them first. We will openly discuss the matter and come to a decision."

Sathyanarayana agreed and said, "You are right. It is better you go alone." Satyanarayana then started talking about their village politics and other family matters. Continuing their conversation, they proceeded to Subbayyamma's house.

When the news was announced that Kodandaramayya is going to study law, Subbayamma and both her sons were very happy. Kodandaramayya sensed a kind of respect in everyone's eyes; he felt 'maybe my decision is not wrong.' He touched Subbayamma's feet and took her blessings. He stayed back at Subbayamma's house that night along with Satyanarayana and took the early morning bus to Ganapavaram the next day.

He reached home by 9 a.m. He saw his mother entering the kitchen after her bath to start cooking. There was no breakfast in those days. Children would drink a glass of milk, and it was very rare that elders would have anything at all in the morning. Everyone normally had their meal before noon. They only had two meals. No mention of tea or coffee in their house at that time. As he was opening the gate, Subbamma saw her son, her eyes lit up, and she came toward him and said, "Nayana, you are here! Good, good. You are finally a college graduate now. Take rest and relax before you start a job. Let me heat up some milk and bring it."

She turned toward her younger daughter, who was standing there, and said, "Give water to Annayya to wash his feet. Why are you standing like a doll?" and hurried inside the kitchen to bring him some milk.

Kodandaramayya said, "Amma, I am not a guest. Why are you scolding her?" looking at Sita, he said, "Looks like amma is too excited to see me." Both the sisters smiled. Everyone's face lit up seeing Kodandaramayya as they thought he is back at home after successfully completing his graduation.

Sita quickly walked to the backyard to tell her father. Sriramulu was cleaning the cowshed after milking the buffalo. Cows were not very common in that area; it was buffaloes that were more prevalent. Sita said, looking at her father, "Annayya is here, come quickly."

Sriramulu looked at her and said, "Ok, let me finish this work and I will be there soon." He never leaves any work halfway unless something very urgent comes up. When Sita turned back to go into the house, she saw Kodandaramayya walking toward them with a glass of milk in his hand. Sriramulu looked at his son affectionately and said, "Ha! Nayana, you are here. Go inside and talk to your mother. I am coming. Why to drink your milk with the smell of cow dung here.

Both siblings smiled at each other and went inside the house. Kodandaramayya started talking to his sister. Sita always had many questions for her brother about the places he went to, and about the schools and colleges.

Sriramulu came in, wiping his wet hands. Looking at Kodandaramayya, he said, "You wrote to me that you will look for jobs before coming. What happened? Could you meet anyone?" Not that I am rushing you."

Kodandaramayya said, "I tried, Nanna, but somehow things did not work out the way I expected. Let us talk after lunch. I will rest for a bit and then take a walk." Looking at his son Sriramulu said, "you have successfully completed your degree. We are all happy. I am sure, one of these days, you will get a job. Don't worry."

Both the parents and sisters tried to draw their own conclusions. His younger sister thought, 'Why is Nanna bothering Annayya? He just came. Give him some time.' The older sister thought, "Annayya has so much responsibility on his shoulders. All of us are dependent on him. Hope God will help him." Subbamma thought, 'Hope all will be okay and that he gets a job soon, so we get out of all our struggles.' She further thought, 'It may be selfish of me to think this way, but what other choice do I have? We are all dependent on him. Things would have been different if Krishna, my younger son, would have been alive. He would have certainly shared the responsibility.' She silently prayed to God to take care of her son.

Sriramulu, having total faith in his son, didn't think much. He just thought, "Why did I blurt out and enquire about a job? Hope I didn't cause my son any pain. Looks like he does not have a positive response. He knows what is right, and he will tell us whenever he is ready," and walked into the backyard to feed the buffaloes some green grass. Around 11 o'clock, after puja and offering food to God, Sriramulu and Kodanda sat down to have their lunch. The girls sometimes ate with their father. As their brother was giving company to their father, they said that they were not hungry , and they would eat later with their mother. Whenever Kodanda was home, after finishing his meal along with his father, he would sit with his mother while she ate, and both of them chatted away.

That day, after finishing his meal along with his father, Kodanda went and sat in the front veranda with a book in his hand. No one talked. The girls quietly had their lunch along with their mother. After finishing their meal, the older daughter said, "Amma, you go and talk to Annayya; he seems a little agitated. I will clean up."

Subbamma nodded her head and, after finishing her meal, went and sat with her son and said, "Nayana, what is bothering you? You look so preoccupied. Tell us what is on your mind."

She then called her husband, who was tending to the bitter gourd creeper. Subbamma got up and brought some cotton and sat down to make wicks for lighting the lamps. She never sat without doing anything. She had to make 365 wicks with cotton to light on the auspicious day of Karthika pournami (the full moon day in the month of November), apart from lighting lamps every day.

Looking at her, Kodandaramayya thought, 'My parents can never sit without doing some work or the other. Both are the same in this matter.' Sriramulu, also came and sat next to Kodanda. Looking at his parents, Kodanda said, "I contacted a few people for jobs. It is not as easy as I thought. We all thought that as soon as I become a graduate, jobs will line up for me. The situation is not very good. The country is settling down after independence, but it is not easy for our national leaders to form the government; so many issues to take care of. Both the British and our national leaders are very nervous. It will take a while for things to settle down."

Subbamma stopped Kodanda, giving a typical mother's advice, and said, "Don't worry, nana, these things take longer than we think. We are in a hurry, but not the employers. There will also be the influence of the stars. We should check it out too. Grahabalam (placing of stars according to the horoscope) also plays a role. We should have faith in God and pray."

Sriramulu said, smiling, "You have a degree now. All these efforts will not go to waste."

Then Subbamma catching up, said, "Is it for this, that you are so nervous and serious? Now relax and spend some time with us; we will ask Satyavathi to come. After some time, you can go and try again. There are so many towns, somewhere or the other, you will get a job."

Saying so, she was about to get up to attend to her work. Kodandaramayya said, "Amma, both of you are ever supporting me. You never find fault or get upset with me. Always making me feel better. Now please listen to me fully." Sriramulu, looking at his wife, said, "You are ever in a hurry for some work or the other."

She sat down and said, "Ok, OK, don't start now."

Kodandaramayya, looking at his father, said, "Nanna, after considering this present situation carefully, I have come to a decision to study law and become an advocate."

Subbamma and Sriramulu did not say anything immediately. This had come as a big surprise to them. They never thought of further studies. Getting a B Com degree is the furthest, they had considered.

Sriramulu recovered first, smiled, and said, "Nayana, are you not satisfied with so many years of studying? You still want to study?"

Kodandaramayya said, "That's not the point, Nanna," and slowly and patiently explained all the reasons for him to opt to study law. He said, "By going into a profession, many doors will open. I can practice law on my own. No one needs to give me a job. Depending on my caliber, I can earn as much. I can even take up a job while practicing law. Law is a respectful and noble profession. Once you are a good lawyer, there will be a possibility to even become a judge," he said with a wistful smile.

When he looked at his father, he thought, 'For the first time, I saw my father with an uncertain look on his face.' Sriramulu was thinking about what Kodandaramayya said. 'Lawyers will be elevated to the bench,' suddenly Sriramulu's face lit up. Looking at his wife, he said, "Now I understand how things are falling into place. When Kodanda was born and I got his horoscope made, it was written in his horoscope that he will have *Mudhra Adhikaram*, which means one will hold a position where he has the authority to stamp on official documents."

Looking at Kodandaramayya, he said, "Good, Nanna, go ahead and continue your studies. We have managed so far; we will manage now. Let us see what is to be done."

He got up and put a hand on his son affectionately and walked out. Kodandaramayya said, "Nanna, where are you going? Rest for a bit." Sriramulu waving his hand went out. Kodandaramayya looked at his mother who was very quiet all this while and said, "Amma, you are not saying anything!" Subbamma, slowly said, "Did you talk to Satyavathi your wife? Can you take her with you?" Kodandaramayya thought, 'Oh, amma is worried for her daughter-in-law.' He said, "I just mentioned to her that there is a possibility that I might go to study law, the last time I met her. Once we decide I will write a letter to her father or I myself will go and talk to them," He then added, "Amma, I understand if you are worried. After thinking a lot and considering all the facts, I came to this decision.

Two more years of difficulties, and we will all be in a better situation," he further added, "Amma, these two years will pass quickly." Subbamma with a lot of pain in her voice said, "When you went to Mylavaram, I felt I would not be able to see you every day, but thought, okay, if I miss him, I can walk and go. I don't need anyone's help. I sent you to Vijayawada. I told myself, "My son had to go for further education; I cannot be selfish. Many youngsters leave their parents to go and study for their betterment. It is still not that far. I can still see him frequently. Then you went to Visakhapatnam, I became a bit more selfish and thought my son will get a degree, and I will be the mother of a degree holder. No one among our relatives have come this far in studies. I thought you will get a better job, and our financial problems will be solved. Although my heart aches to put so much burden on you. Do I have any choice? Your father is aging. Both these girls are growing up. What can I do? Now I don't understand your decision. You still want to study. You have a wife. What will her family think? Letting her stay on at her parent's place for so long after marriage."

Subbamma asked with a frustrated voice, "Do you have to go back to Vishakhapatnam? Can you not study in Vijayawada? How long will it take to complete?"

Kodandaramayya smiled. He came close to her, put a hand on her shoulder, and said, "Amma, I have to go to Madras. I cannot study law anywhere else. It will take 2 years to get the law degree and one year for apprenticeship. During the apprenticeship, I will be able to earn some money. Amma, please try to understand. Don't get agitated."

Subbamma looked like the sky had fallen on her head. She said, "Then you can push me into the river Krishna and go, I can't take it any more. You are going that far and for so long."

Somehow, when certain words are uttered consciously or unconsciously, depending on the time and the mindset of the people involved, the situation becomes explosive and dramatic. This particular sentence Subbamma uttered, Kodandaramayya took it so seriously and was deeply hurt. He immediately withdrew from his mother, got up, and said, "Amma, I am your son. How can you say such things to me? Do you know how difficult it was for me to come to this decision? I thought you would understand." He got up and started walking toward the front yard.

Subbamma was shocked at the words of her son. She could not utter a word and quietly looked at her son. Then she saw her husband walking in. She heard him asking his son, "Where are you going, Nayana?"

Kodanda said, "Just for a walk. I will walk till our farm and will be back soon," and walked away. Sriramulu asked Subbamma, "What happened to Nayana? He looks troubled. Did you say anything to hurt him?"

Looking at his wife, he was about to say something, but with one glance at her face, he understood that she was already feeling bad. He checked himself and said in a mild voice, "You must have said something. Think before saying anything. He wants to go for further studies. He is not shunning his responsibilities like many youngsters these days, joining the independence movement, leaving their families, or going and acting in dramas and cinemas. Now, go and prepare some snacks; none of us ate properly at lunch."

He went out again. Subbamma was worried and thought, 'Where is he going again?' She got up to attend to her work, thinking, 'What have I done? Hurt my son who is everything to me!'

After finishing his work, Sriramulu also went to the farm. He saw his son there walking along the fencing of the farm. Looking at his father, he said, "Oh, Nanna, why did you come all the way? I am coming home." Sriramulu did not say anything. They both walked home in silence. It was almost dinner time. They all had a quiet dinner and went to bed early. Everyone was tired, and engrossed in their own thoughts.

Next day for lunch, Subbamma made Garelu (lentil dumplings), Kodanda's favourite. The girls said, "Annayya, amma never makes these even if we ask or during festivals. She says, 'Your Annayya likes them, how can I make them when he is not here?"

Kodanda smiled and said, "Amma loves me more than you, that's why." To that, all laughed, and somehow the atmosphere became light. The girls cleaned up after the meals so Subbamma could have her meal. As Subbamma started to eat, Kodanda sat with her to keep her company as usual. Subbamma, stopped mixing the rice, looked at her son and said, "Nayana, I hurt you by saying things without thinking. I could not bear the thought of you going away again and also Satyavathi staying away from you after the marriage for so long. Don't hold this in your heart."

Kodanda looked at her and said, "Amma, I do understand. Now, have your lunch. Everything will be fine." He got up and walked into the front yard. Subbamma thought, 'he still did not get over it.' True enough, Kodanda never forgot that incident. Even later in his life, he would often bring it up, saying to his mother, "Remember what you said when I wanted to go to do law? You said, push me into the river Krishna and go."

To that, Subbamma would say, "How long do you want to hold on to it and remind me?"

Like a child, Kodanda would repeat and say, "Did you say that or not?"

She would get irritated and yell at him, saying, "Enough is enough now." Kodanda would laugh, and seeing that, she would also laugh and say, "Now, go from here," with pretended anger.

The next day, after lunch, Sriramulu asked, "When do you have to go back, Kodanda?"

Kodanda said, "I will have to go back in a couple of days, to apply for the seat. Once it is confirmed, I have to look for accommodation and will come back. Then, I have 20 days before joining the college. I will ask your daughter-in-law to come and join us." The girls were happy that their sister-in-law would be coming. The rest of the day was uneventful.

The next day, Sriramlu asked Kodanda, "Nayana, how much money will you require now?"

To this, Kodanda said, "Nanna, I am not sure. Now I just need some money for my travel. I have to first put in my application. After that, once I procure a seat in the college, I have to pay some amount as admission fees. I will look for a humble accommodation and see how much it costs. I will write a letter to you. Now I am not sure at all. We will have some time. Please, don't stress yourself. I will also see if I can arrange some money."

Sriramulu, thought, 'Anyway, I will have to start working around it.'

Kodanda left a couple of days after that. He then proceeded to Kalavakuru to meet his wife and his in-laws. Satyavathi felt happy and proud that her husband came to visit her. She felt he missed her and cared for her. Her sister-in-law teased her, saying, "See, your husband came running to see you without staying long at Ganapavaram." Satyavathi smiled confidently, thinking that the constant traveling between her mother's place and her mother-in-law's place had finally come to an end.

Kodandaramayya stayed there for 3 days. His father-in-law was expecting him to say something about his future plans. The day before he left, that night Kodandaramayya said to Satyavathi that he tried hard to get a job but was not happy with the way things were going. He then mentioned that he was thinking of studying law, seeing it as the best option for an independent life and not having to work for anyone. He explained that law was a profession taken up by many freedom fighters and had good prospects. He narrated the incident at Guntur and his job search efforts. Finally, after explaining everything, he said, "Hope you understand my predicament. It will take me two more years."

He also suggested that Satyavathi could come and stay at Ganapavaram if she felt uncomfortable staying at her mother's place after marriage for extended periods. He told her if she could come to Vijayawada, he would pick her up on his way back to Ganapavaram from Madras. He will be in Ganapavaram throughout the summer holidays. It took a while for Satyavathi to digest this new information. She nodded her head and said, "Just let me know when I have to join you in Vijayawada." Kodandaramayya wondered, "How much pain am I causing her with this decision?"

Next morning, when the whole family was together, he told them that he had decided to study law and that he was heading to Madras to apply and procure a seat in law. His father-in-law didn't understand what was going on with his son-in-law. He thought about how long this boy would carry on studying. He was married and also has the responsibility of his own family. Thinking this, he asked Kodandaramayya, "Did your parents agree?" Kodandaramayya smiled and said, "How can I do this without their consent? I have their blessings." Satyanarayana could not say anything. His brother-in-law said after a few minutes, "That is good, Kodandaramayya. Wish you all the best." Kodandaramayya left after lunch, saying that he would write a letter when he reached Vijayawada on his way back from Madras. If Satyavathi could join him there they would all go to Ganapavaram and spend the holidays there before going to Madras to join the university. All settled he proceeded to Vijayawada.

Satyavathi being the youngest child of her parents and with a brother much older than her, was treated with lots of love and tenderness. She adored her brother and her sister-in-law.

By nature, she was also a very docile and adjusting girl. She and her sister-in-law had a loving, intimate relationship. She was the darling of the family. Her older sister and brother-in-law also treated her like their daughter.

She felt that her father was not very happy with this situation. She thought, 'My husband has decided to study further. It will be difficult for me, actually for all of us – for him, his family, and my family too. But if he becomes a lawyer, won't we all feel proud? Nothing comes easy. What he is doing is for the family. I don't need to analyse much; he is my husband, and I will support him.'

She walked into the backyard with a certain determination and saw her father talking to her mother. She thought, 'Oh, father is explaining to amma and Vadina.' They all looked at her. Her father, turning to her, said, "Satyavathi, it will take two or even three years for Kodandaramayya to finish his studies. You may not be able to join him before he finishes."

Satyavathi said, "It is okay, Nanna. He wants to study further, which is a good thing. I want to go to Ganapavaram. I will join him in Vijayawada when he is returning from Madras, which may be in four or five days. From now on, I will spend more time in Ganapavaram. He will be visiting the family often there. Please make the arrangements.

She said this with finality in her voice, looking at her brother. Her brother looked at her and said lovingly, "Ok, Satyam, let us look for an auspicious day. Your sister-in-law and I will come and drop you in Ganapavaram."

Her sister-in-law, looking at her mother-in-law said "I am going to soak some rice for the snacks. Let us make some ariselu," (a favourite sweet dish in the family, also a custom to send along with the daughter when she goes to her in-laws' house).

Satyavathi's mother said, "Great news, Kodandaramayya is going to be a lawyer. This boy has the determination to pursue higher studies." Looking at her daughter, she said, "You are right, you must go now and be with him." Looking at her son, she said, "Ask our purohit (family priest) for a good day."

She looked at Satyavathi and said, "Ok, now go and soak 2 kg of rice."

Satyavathi looked at her mother enquiringly and walked away thinking, 'My mother never gives me any work. She is asking me to do this to take my mind off.' And smiled to herself.

Satyanarayana, her father, walked away a little irritated about the whole situation. He was hoping that Kodandaramayya would settle down soon. He was thinking, 'They have no property, where will they find the money? There are a lot of responsibilities on his shoulders. His father, who is the sole earning member, is getting old. Why is he not taking up a job? But after listening to his wife, he unconsciously felt a tinge of pride and thought, 'Well, if he is interested in further studies which may improve his future prospects and he has his parents, approval, why should I object?' Thinking this way, he walked away to attend to his work.

A week later, when Narasimha Rao, Satyavathi's brother, received a letter from Kodandaramayya telling them when he would be reaching Vijayawada. Satyavathi, accompanied by her sister-in-law and her brother, went to Vijayawada a day before Kodandaramayya arrived. Kodandaramayya told them that all had gone well, and he could secure a seat in Law. They all spent a day at Subbayyamma's house enjoying each other's company. Kodandaramayya held Satyavathi's sister-in-law, Sakuntal, in high regard. He insisted that his brother-in-law and Sakuntala should go to Ganapavarm to spend a couple of days with them, before returning to their village.

They all proceeded to Ganapavarm the next day. Satyavathi was happy that her brother and sister-in-law were coming with her to her in-law's house.

The whole family spent a few days together. The girls were very happy that both their brother and sister-in-law were with them at the same time.

Subbamma would not stop making various delicious snacks for the children. It was a joyous time for the family. Sriramulu also relaxed a bit.

Kodandaramayya took over all the chores of his father. Cleaning the barn, filling water tubs from the well for the day's use. He liked watering the plants, fertilising the soil with manure, and removing the weeds. In the evening, he would teach his sisters. Only after dinner, Satyavathi would finally get some time alone with her husband.

Once he was organizing his father's cupboard filled with papers, he came across a small notebook where his father wrote down the monthly expenses. When he saw the cost of a matchbox, wicks for the kerosene lamp, noted along with the bigger essential items like rice, dal, oil, etc., he was surprised and admired the astute mind of his father and thought, 'There is always something to keep learning from my father.'

When the time came for her son to leave, Subbamma prepared and packed all kinds of snacks for her son to take along. Satyavathi quietly helped her mother-in-law in all the chores with a heavy heart, but without a sigh, complaint, or showing any sort of emotion, since it was not one of her traits.

Subbamma would always say, "Nothing can shake my daughter-in-law's composure." Though Satyavathi was the youngest and most pampered in her parents' house, she was never a spoiled child. She gained a reputation among all her relatives that 'Satyavathi is a personification of endurance, a girl with a lot of dignity, and one who never complains.' Although there was a big difference between her parents' house and her in-laws' house monetarily, she never once told or complained to anyone about any of her struggles. Such was her self-respect and the respect for the family she married into.

Sriramulu quietly gave some money to his son before he left. Kodanda asked, "Nanna, how did you manage this money?"

Sriramulu smiled and said, "Don't worry. Go and study well and fulfil your goals. That is the most important thing right now."

Kodanda's affection for his father grew and he thought, 'Generosity and wisdom. That is what my father is.'

The day arrived when Kodandaramayya had to leave. Kodanda went to his sisters and said, "Do study well, and take care of Amma and Nanna."

He had to take the first bus to Mylavaram at 7 in the morning, and from there, he had to take another bus to Vijayawada. There, he had to board a train to Madras, which would reach early in the morning the following day. The girls were going to miss his presence since he gave them a sense of security and protection. Their father was getting old, so it was their brother who was always the guardian and a well-wisher, taking great care of them.

Subbamma felt sad that her son alone was bearing the weight of the whole family. When she thought she hurt her son with her senseless anxiety, she felt sad and guilty. For Sriramulu, nothing in the world mattered more than his son and his welfare.

Satyavathi was, of course, going through a mixture of feelings. She was proud of her husband, on whom everybody depended, and nobody else she knew in her big family bravely ventured for higher studies.

Her role at her parents' house was very different from here. There, she was a little princess, always pampered by all and carefree, with no responsibilities. But here, she was the only daughter-in-law, and all her husband's responsibilities automatically came onto her shoulders.

She had to be there with her husband in every act and support him. All her family and relatives wondered how she was going to take such a big responsibility of the whole family, but she thought, 'I will not oppose my husband in any way, and I will simply support and follow him.' And she truly did adhere to this until the very end.

The whole family walked with Kodandaramayya till the gate when he was leaving. Satyavathi stood back in the verandah, while Subbamma and the girls walked with him till the gate. Kodandaramayya, without turning back, said, "Okay now," and walked quickly accompanied by his father who was going to the bus stand along with him. As he walked, he did not think about anyone or anything and focused on his journey. Being present in moment is what he did.

He reached Vijayawada around 11 o'clock and went straight to Gurunatha Rao's place. Gurunatha Rao was very happy to see Kodandaramayya. Looking at him, he understood that Kodanda was on his way to Madras and that his parents agreed to let him go for his further studies. He welcomed his cousin with open arms and asked, "When do you have to leave for Madras?"

Kodanda said, "I am thinking of taking the afternoon train." Gurunatha Rao said, "Okay, now let's go and see Akkayya. You can have lunch, and I will drop you at the station. Let me finish seeing my patients, and we will go."

Kodandaramayya sat down and pondered over the events of the past few days. He thought about how so much had happened so quickly in the past few days and also thought, 'Hope my decision is not wrong. I have considered all the facts before making this decision.' He quickly dismissed the thoughts, thinking, 'Why these thoughts now? I have to focus, work hard, and quickly reach my goals to relieve my father of his cares.' He then closed his eyes and tried to rest.

Gurunatha Rao, after wrapping up his work, came out and said to him, "Come, let's go." And they headed to Subbayamma's house.

It was 1 o'clock. Subbayamma was happy to see Kodandaramayya as usual and said, "Nayana, so you are off to Madras to become an advocate. We are all very happy. Come, wash up, and I will serve in 10 minutes." Then she asked, "When do you go to Madras?" Kodanda said, "I have to take the afternoon train."

She then said, "I will pack some dinner to take with you on the train. Don't eat outside food," and she walked hurriedly into the kitchen. Kodandaramayya was touched by seeing the love, affection, and happiness that all of them were showing toward him.

Kodanda suddenly remembered Sriramamurthy and Ramachandrudu, who were his mentors. It had been a while since he saw them. He thought, 'How can I forget the affection and encouragement they showered upon me?' He decided spontaneously that he would go meet them, take their blessings, and catch the train the next afternoon.

He immediately shared his plan with Gurunatha Rao and Subbayamma who was in the kitchen. "Akkayya, you don't have to hurry and trouble yourself. Please take your time and finish your work. I am not leaving today. I will leave tomorrow." Subbayamma turned and looked at both Gurunatha Rao and Kodanda and asked, "What happened? Why the sudden change of plans?"

Kodanda explained that he had to meet Sriramamurthy and Ramchandrudu and seek their blessings. Subbayamma smiled and said, "That's very good! You must do that. You always do the right thing. All my blessings to you," and turned away with tears in her eyes. Kodandaramayya was touched by her genuine love and affection for him.

After lunch, Kodandaramayya headed to Sriramamurthy's house. He told Gurunatha Rao that he would stay the night with Subbayamma and come and see him the next day and go to the railway station from there. Gurunatha Rao nodded and said, "Yes, that's a good plan. I will see you tomorrow. You can spend some time with Akkayya and the boys today."

Kodandaramayya headed first to Sriramamurthy 's house since it was closer to Subbayamma's house. It was 2 o'clock in the afternoon, and Vijayawada's sun was quite hot. He thought that he would spend some time there, and by then, it would cool down. He could then walk to Ramachandrudu 's house.

It never entered his head to take a rickshaw. The great walker, he walked everywhere. When he reached their house, he saw Sriramamurthy having his afternoon cup of coffee. Janakamma, his wife, was also present. He went straight to them and touched their feet with reverence. Sriramamurthy was overwhelmed looking at Kodanda and said, "How are you, Kodandaramayya? Did you finish your B. Com? Sit down. When did you come? Tell me everything. It has been a while since I last saw you."

Kodandaramayya said, "Yes, I am sorry I haven't come to visit you. Please forgive me." Sriramamurthy smiled and said, "No, no it is alright. All that is not necessary. Sit down and tell me."

Janakamma was also very happy to see Kodandaramayya. She got up and went inside and handed him a glass of buttermilk and said, "Let me make something for you to eat. You must've walked from wherever you're coming, all the way here."

Kodandaramayya said, "No, Amma, I am okay. Please don't trouble yourself." Then, he turned toward Sriramamurthy and explained how he has decided to go pursue law after his B.Com, why he has taken this decision, and how his family had approved and was supporting this pursuit.

After the whole narration, Sriramamurthy looked at Kodandaramayya and said, "It's very good, Nayana. I am very happy that you have become a graduate and now you are pursuing law! It is, of course, a noble profession. You don't have to work for anyone. Many of the freedom fighters are lawyers for that reason. They didn't want to work for the Britishers." Kodandaramayya thought, "How nice, he is also thinking on the same lines as I am" and felt reassured.

Sriramamurthy also inquired about Kodandaramayya's family. He asked if his father had agreed to further studies. Kodandaramayya said that his entire family has supported his decision. Without it, he would not have been able to pursue this path. Sriramamurthy said, "Do take good care of your wife. She seems to be a very nice girl. Not fussing about being away from you." Kodanda nodded his head and smiled. After a while, Kodanda took his leave, saying, "I will go and meet Ramchandrudu Master. I am leaving for Madras tomorrow."

He touched the couple's feet with reverence and left.

As he was reaching Ramchandrudu 's house, it was twilight. The lights were switched on in the houses as well as on the streets. He could hear bells ringing while evening pujas were performed in the temples. Kodandaramayya walked with a smile on his face as he absorbed all this with a feeling of nostalgia.

When he reached Ramchandrudu 's house, his wife came out and, seeing Kodandaramayya, said, "Oh, it is you, Kodandaramayya, come, come. Please sit. How are you? You forgot us. How long has it been! You haven't visited us." She showered him with questions. Kodandaramayya did pranam to her and then said, "Yes, Amma. You are right. I should have come and visited you. But I couldn't make it earlier." Before he spoke further, she interrupted and said, "It's okay. Now tell me all about you. Oh, by the way, your Master garu is not here. He went to a meeting. Some freedom fighter is giving a speech. You know about him; he is always interested in all these things. He may be late by the time he comes back home."

Kodandaramayya said, "I have completed my B.Com and am now applying for Law in Madras. I am leaving tomorrow for Madras tomorrow. I have come to inform you, and take your blessings."

She smiled and said, "Very happy, Nayana. You have succeeded with hard work and sincerity. Your parents are fortunate and must be so proud of you." Kodandaramayya with reverence said, "Amma, it is the blessing of you all," and stood up to take his leave." She said hurriedly, "Wait, wait! I made some payasam (milk pudding). You cannot leave without eating. Your guru will get upset. On top of that, you have given me good news too."

She hurried into the kitchen and came out with a bowl of payasam. Kodandaramayya happily relished the payasam and started walking toward the familiar tap to wash it. She, looked at him with affection, said, "Nayana! You don't have to do that. It's not like those days when you used to be a student and lived here. Now give it to me," saying so she forcefully grabbed the bowl from his hand. Kodandaramayya humbly said, "Amma, I am the same person even now. I will always be a student and your child. Nothing has changed." She then said with a smile, "I know, I know, you have always been a humble boy." Kodandaramayya then took leave, saying that he will be back to see Master garu. As he walked toward the gate, he thought, "I am blessed to receive so much love from people around me."

By the time he returned to Subbayamma's house, it was almost dinner time. The rest of the evening went by quickly. After having dinner, he chatted a bit with Subbayamma's sons and went to bed. All of them slept on jute cots in the verandah, with a bed sheet on top and another sheet to cover themselves. Except for a couple of months during winter, everyone slept outside in the veranda. Vijayawada hardly sees any real winter.

After finishing his morning chores, Kodandaramayya went to Subbayamma and said, "Akkayya, I have to leave now. I will go to Durga temple, and from there, I will go to see Gurunatha Rao. The railway station is close to his place. Gurunatha Rao also said he wants to see me before I head off to Madras." Subbayamma said, "Okay. Go to the temple and come back. You can have your meal and then go. You have to come back anyway to pick up the luggage." Kodandaramayya nodded his head and left.

He then headed towards the temple. Though it was quite a distance, he walked quickly and ran up the steps to the temple, as he always used to do when he lived in Vijayawada. He rarely asked the goddess Durga anything, except for her blessings and grace. He sat on the steps for a minute, quickly came down, and proceeded to Subbayamma's house. She served him a nice, hot meal with affection and gave a him a packed dinner as she had promised. After that, he took her blessings and left for Gurunatha Rao's house.

Gurunatha Rao, seeing Kodandaramayya said, "I have been waiting. What took you so long? I thought I could spend some time with you before you go."

Kodandaramayya smiled and said, "I went to the Durga temple, and then, you know, Akkaya, she won't allow me to leave without having my meal." Gurnatha Rao nodded and said, "Of course. By the way, how was your trip to Sriramamurthy and Ramachandrudu garu?" Kodandaramayya narrated his meetings with them. Gurunatha Rao said, "Okay, good, you did what you wanted to do, and you took their blessings. Now look towards the future."

They chatted for a while and then both headed to the railway station. Gurunatha Rao's cook and attendant also went along with them to the railway station. He quickly got onto the train and found a seat for Kodandaramayya, placed his baggage.

Kodandaramayya bid farewell and said, "I will write as soon as I can." Gurunatha Rao said, "Don't worry about anything now," and patted Kodandaramayya's back affectionately.

As the train commenced its journey, he reflected, "Another chapter unfolds in my life." and a smile graced his lips. Kodandaramayya found himself deep in contemplation about his decision to pursue legal education. Doubt crept into his mind as he pondered, "I trust I'm not making a mistake." Recollections of his father's own daunting life choices surfaced. His father had left behind his beloved village, property, and cherished relationships to start anew in a distant land, displaying remarkable courage and resilience.

Ever since he made the decision to study the Law, Kodandaramayya's journey of self-discovery had commenced. Each experience became a lesson, teaching him to move forward without dwelling on the past, a trait he inherited from his father. His father had left Modepally to carve out a life in Ganapavaram and never glanced back after settling legal matters. Kodandaramayya, too, embraced this philosophy. He absorbed the lessons life presented, then released them, refusing to dwell on what had passed.

Kodandaramayya shook off these thoughts, reminding himself of the thorough consideration he had given to his own decision. His family stood firmly behind him, offering unwavering support. Determined to forge ahead and succeed, he closed his eyes, seeking solace as the train accelerated its pace.

When the train stopped after a while, he looked out and saw that the station was Ongole. Immediately, a number of thoughts rushed to his mind, reminding him of his childhood. His father hails from a small village near Ongole, and how, overnight, he made a decision and migrated to Ganapavaram in Krishna district. Kodandaramayya's mind slipped into the past.

Parents Sriramulu and Subbamma

Chapter 2
EARLY BEGINNINGS

The family traced its roots back to 1426 CE during the reign of Proudha Deva Raya of Vijayanagar kings. One of the courtiers, Tamarapalli Abbayya Mantri, a great writer of his time, impressed King Proudha Devaraya with his writings. He was gifted with the Paidi Gantam, a writing instrument made of gold. People used to write with gantams on palm leaves before paper was ever made. Thereafter, the family's name changed from Tamarapalli to Paidigantam, later becoming popular as Pamidighantam. Their ancestors hail from the village Tamarapalli near Ramachandrapuram in East Godavari District in Andhra Pradesh. Some of the families migrated from Tamarapalli Village due to drought conditions and settled around the river Gundlakamma in the erstwhile Guntur ditrict, near the villages of Anamanamuru, Nannurupadu, Modepally, Perayapalem, and Razanagaram.

Kodandaramayya's father, Sriramulu, hails from the village Modepally in Guntur district (presently within Prakasham district). The family was well-respected in the village. They had fairly large share of farmland. Kodandaramayya's father was the third of four brothers and two sisters. All four brothers were tall and handsome, with imposing personalities. Everyone said that they took after their father, whom they lost at a very young age. Their mother had a tiny frame, she was fair and beautiful. She often warned her sons that not all of them should be present at the same place and at the same time, especially not with her in public, as she was fearful of someone casting a black eye on them.

Sriramulu was forty-one years old, and his mother, Subbamma, was sixteen when Kodandaramayya was born on October 26, 1926, in a small village, Modepally, then in in the Madras presidency (currently part of Prakasham District of Andhra Pradesh).

When the elated parents set eyes on their firstborn with wonder, pride, and a sense of fulfilment, little did they know that this bright-eyed, charming little infant would bring them name and fame, and that he would touch many hearts around him.

His mother, Subbamma, was married at the age of 9, and when she turned 11, she entered her mother-in-law's house. In those days, it was customary to address the husband's house as the mother-in-law's house, even if the mother-in-law was not alive. Both her mother-in-law and father-in-law passed away by the time Subbamma entered that household. The only woman present was her elder brother-in-law's wife, who took Subbamma under her wing and became a mother figure away from her own mother. She taught her everything. Her daughter, who was 4 years younger than Subbamma, became her best friend.

She did not think much about the age difference between her and her husband. Even if it crossed her mind at some point, she accepted it like many other girls of that time, as it was a common practice. She thought, 'My parents married me off to this man, he is my husband, and I have to live with him for the rest of my life.' She hoped that he would cherish her, care for her and her children, give her respect, and treat her with dignity. If he did not, she would have to bear everything and would have to nurture and venerate him and the family.

When she looked at her little son, her heart filled with pride and joy. He looked just like his father, whom she adored. Her husband was a handsome and a courageous man; he was called Guntur Puli (Tiger). When he gave alms to people, he gave to the fullest satisfaction of the receiver. Theirs was an agricultural family. He could work in the fields relentlessly, for he enjoyed hard work. She often thought, "My husband does not know what laziness is."

They did not have to think about the name of their little boy. It was decided even before he was born. When Sriramulu went on a pilgrimage to Tirupathi with his wife after their marriage, he prayed at the famous Kodanda Ramaswamy temple, asking the Lord to bless him with a son. If his wish was granted, he would name his son after the Lord Kodanda Rama. It is a famous Sri Rama temple mentioned in the Varaha Purana that Srirama, along with Sita Devi and Lakshmana, stopped there for some time while they were returning from Lanka. It is believed that the Lord Rama here grants all the wishes of devotees when asked sincerely.

His parents affectionately addressed him as Nayana. Nayana, in the Telugu language, means father. In many households, it is customary to address one's son as Nayana and daughter as Amma, that is, mother. It reflects the love and affection for the parents and a feeling that the parents are never out of their minds. In fact, many times people address the young ones as Nayana and Amma to show affection. Kodandaramayya became Kodanda to his near and dear.

Both of Kodanda's paternal aunts got married and lived in distant villages, so their visits to their mother's home were rare. The older aunt and her family became close to Kodanda at a later time. Kodanda's youngest uncle, Kamayya, who was unmarried when he was growing up, took care of his nephew and always carried him wherever he went. From the time Kodanda turned a year old, he would sleep with his uncle, eat with him, and his uncle would never let him leave his side. He was, of course, Kodanda's favourite. The father, at times, felt a bit irritated at not getting enough of his son, but then would brush it off thinking, 'Who is he? My own brother,' and would smile to himself.

Kodanda didn't mingle much with children of his age. He would tag along with his mother while she was attending to the household chores and listened to her stories, for Subbamma was a great storyteller. At other times he would often run after his uncle and father to the fields and play on his own in nature.

Kodanda's younger brother, Krishna, was born when he turned three years of age. Subbamma was content and thought; 'Now I am the mother of two children, a grown woman.' Looking at her little one, she thought, 'This child looks more like me,' and smiled to herself with satisfaction. Sriramulu thought, 'I have a son again; maybe I will be blessed like my parents with 4 sons and 2 daughters.' His prediction regarding the daughters came true. At a very late age, the couple were indeed blessed with 2 daughters.

One evening, Kodanda accompanied his father to the fields as Sriramulu wanted to inspect the day's work after the workers had left. While surveying the fields, Sriramulu spontaneously lifted Kodanda onto his shoulders, proudly declaring, "Nayana, all these paddy fields you see belong to us." Kodanda felt a trace of pride and satisfaction in his father's tone but didn't fully grasp the significance, so he quickly hopped down and went to play at the nearby pond. Sriramulu chuckled at his son's innocence and continued walking.

Sriramulu's second brother, who worked in Guntur, would occasionally visit Modepally to collect the produce. This would sometimes irk the brothers at home who felt resentful as they were the ones who worked hard all year, while their brother seemed to just come and take his share. However, they never voiced their frustrations as it was an unspoken rule in joint families.

The family enjoyed a respected status in the village, owning a substantial amount of land. However, like numerous other villagers, they grappled with a lack of ready cash. This financial shortfall presented hurdles, particularly when facing major expenses like organizing family weddings or scaling up their farming activities. In such circumstances, they frequently turned to moneylenders for loans, who imposed steep interest rates. Struggling to fulfil these financial obligations, many landowners found themselves compelled to sell their land at meagre prices, resulting in substantial losses. Only those who possessed savvy business skills were able to protect their assets amid these economic challenges.

Despite thinking that everything was under control, the family soon realized otherwise. With all the brothers married and responsible for their own families, the family's property began to dwindle. Each brother would borrow money for their individual needs, leading to a cycle of debt. When creditors came knocking, they had no choice but to part with parcels of land, since there was no income to cover expenses. Unfortunately, the brothers sometimes gave the same piece of land to multiple creditors inadvertently, leading to scandalous situations.

Sriramulu, known for his integrity, found the situation unbearable. He couldn't stand the thought of losing his dignity and living amidst such turmoil. He concluded that he couldn't carry on living in such circumstances. Feeling that he had reached his limit, Sriramulu decided it was time to leave the village and seek out a new path for himself and his family.

The atmosphere at home had become tense, with the brothers communicating only when necessary and lacking any casual conversation. This strained dynamics deeply troubled the women of the household, leaving them unsure of how to navigate their relationships.

Kodanda fell ill and was down with fever one day. His beloved uncle, who usually never left his side, did not come to see him right away. When he eventually came, bent over his nephew and asked, "Nayana, how are you feeling? You've got a fever?" Kodanda gave him a stern look and slapped his uncle on the cheek, saying, "Oh, finally you came now to see me!" with tears in his eyes. His uncle was taken aback, rubbing his cheek. He said, "I know you are upset with me," pain dripping from his voice. He said, "Times are bad and my fate too," and walked away. His cousin sister, who bathed him, fed him, and played with him, became aloof. This broke his heart.

Despite hoping for reconciliation and understanding among the brothers, Sriramulu waited patiently for a couple of months, but things did not improve. He realized that the rift had grown too deep to mend, and he contemplated leaving. The only place he could think of was his sister's village in the Krishna district near Vijayawada. Sriramulu's brother-in-law, a respected and wealthy figure who served as the village head, seemed like the only beacon of hope. Sriramulu believed that seeking guidance from him would offer him a chance to rebuild his life with dignity.

When Sriramulu mentioned his plan to seek help from his younger sister's household to his wife, she was horrified. She expressed her disapproval, stating that it was against custom to turn to one's younger sister for assistance, especially in difficult times. According to tradition, one is expected to provide for their younger sister, not the other way around. However, when Subbamma conveyed her concerns to her husband, he brushed them aside, asserting that he didn't seek her opinion or permission. He also suggested that she didn't fully grasp the gravity of the situation, despite his explanation.

Subbamma couldn't help but felt a sense of resignation as she realized that discord had crept into her life as well. She understood that in times of turmoil, it was often the wife who bore the brunt of blame and irritation from her husband. Reflecting on this, she recognized that her journey through life was about to take a new, and perhaps challenging, turn.

Despite the heartfelt pleas from villagers who respected and admired Sriramulu, urging him not to leave and assuring him of their support, Sriramulu remained practical and cognizant of the harsh realities of life. While he appreciated their sentiment, he pondered the limitations of their assistance. He knew that while they might stand by him in solidarity, they couldn't restore his lost lands, nor could he rely on their support indefinitely. As he waited for a month, attempting to reconcile with his brothers without success, Sriramulu recognized that there seemed to be no viable solution in sight. Ultimately, he made the difficult decision to depart quietly.

That evening after dinner, her husband's unexpected announcement left her stunned. His instructions to pack up and leave at dawn, without causing any commotion, sent shockwaves through her. He further said that we will first go to Bodduvane Palem, inform your parents and leave for Chandrala. She was happy that her husband considered informing her parents.

Inside, the palpable tension weighed heavily on her. The silence from her family members only amplified her distress. Their unspoken acknowledgment of the impending departure pierced her heart. Questions swirled in her mind, wondering why her usually supportive sister-in-law and her daughter remained silent. Their lack of response added to her anguish, planting seeds of doubt about their ability to survive in their current environment.

Wiping away tears of frustration and sadness, she mechanically gathered a few belongings, clinging to the precious items gifted by her family. Exhausted both physically and emotionally, she sought solace next to her sleeping sons. Yet, sleep eluded her. Her mind consumed by the uncertainties of the future and the weight of her husband's decision.

As dawn approached, she found herself torn between resignation and determination. Despite her inner turmoil, she resolved to stand by her husband's side, clinging to the hope that their departure would lead to a better life. With a heavy heart and a mind filled with apprehension, she awaited the dawn of a new chapter in their lives.

In the early hours, her husband's firm yet gentle voice pierced the stillness of the morning, signalling the time to depart. Without hesitation, Subbamma rose swiftly, her mind already racing with thoughts of their impending journey. As she prepared herself for the journey ahead, Subbamma couldn't shake the heaviness in her heart. The prospect of leaving behind their familiar surroundings weighed heavily on her, and tears welled up in her eyes as she quietly lamented the lack of farewells from those they were leaving behind.

Amidst the subdued atmosphere, Subbamma's husband remained stoic, his emotions carefully concealed beneath a facade of composure. His unwavering demeanour both impressed and perplexed her, leaving her to wonder at his seemingly boundless self-control in the face of such upheaval.

Meanwhile, young Kodanda, although unable to fully grasp the complexities of the situation, sensed his father's inner turmoil. Despite his tender age, he admired his father's unwavering resolve and steadfastness. With the bullock cart prepared and their belongings in tow, Subbamma and her family embarked on their journey, leaving behind the familiar comforts of their village in search of a brighter future. Though their departure was met with silence, the bonds of love and resilience that bound them together would carry them forward into the unknown.

As Subbamma and her family arrived at Bodduvane Palem, the tranquil scene of village life unfolded before them. Dawn was breaking, painting the sky with hues of orange and pink, while the gentle sounds of morning rituals filled the air. Women could be seen sprinkling water in front of their houses, creating intricate Muggulu designs with vibrant colours. Nearby, men went about their tasks, some brushing their teeth with neem sticks, while others tended to the cows, milking them in preparation for the day ahead.

As they approached her parents' home, Subbamma's heart swelled with a mix of emotions. The familiar sights and sounds of the village stirred memories of her childhood, filling her with a sense of nostalgia and comfort. It was a stark contrast to the tension and uncertainty that had pained her in recent days.

Her father, engaged in his morning chores, looked up at the sight of the approaching bullock cart. His eyes widened with recognition, and he called out to his wife, anticipating the arrival of one of their daughters. With seven daughters and a son, theirs was another hardworking farming family, deeply rooted in the rhythms of village life.

Subbamma's mother, Sitaravamma, a woman of quiet strength and unwavering dedication, got all her seven daughters married. Despite the challenges they faced, she had worked tirelessly to raise her children and worked very hard to keep the family together. She also has a son, Venkateswarulu, who is the youngest of her children. Ensuring the well-being of all and managing the household, she had shouldered the responsibilities with grace and determination.

She came out to see who had come at that early hour. She was delighted to see her favourite grandsons, her son-in-law, and her daughter. At the same time, she also felt a sense of concern as this son-in law of hers hardly visited them and would only arrive after repeated invitations. Now, what had brought on this sudden visit? She hoped that everything was alright. She quickly helped her daughter to alight from the bullock cart, picked up the younger grandson, while the older one, Kodanda, jumped out of the cart holding his mother's hand.

Sriramulu placed the luggage on the ground and gave some money to the farm helper, Venkayya, who brought them, and asked him to return soon so that he could be home on time to attend to his work. Venkayya, with tears in his eyes, said, "Babayya, come home soon, don't move away forever," and quickly got on to the cart and, without looking back, moved away. Meanwhile, Subbamma's father and her fifteen-year-old brother came out to welcome them. After the preliminary exchange of greetings, Sriramulu, who didn't mince words, came straight to the point and said, "I came to inform you that things are getting worse at home. I cannot live there anymore. I am going to my sister and brother-in-law's place near Vijayawada. With their help, I want to make a life there. I am not leaving my family here; I am taking them along with me."

Subbamma sensed a trace of relief in her parents' faces. Her mother said, "How will you manage there with the family?" In response, Sriramulu said, "My brother-in-law is a capable and helpful person whom I trust. I'm sure he'll be able to do something for me, and I will settle down soon enough."

No one spoke for a while. The father said, "I know your brother-in-law; he has a good reputation, and he is a well-respected person with a good heart. I think you are doing the right thing; I give you all my blessings." Sriramulu said, "We are leaving early tomorrow morning, so that we can reach before it gets dark. We need to change two buses and walk some distance. As I have not informed my sister's family, they will not be able to send a bullock cart for us. I have come to inform you and to take your blessings."

Subbamma felt a tinge of pride in her heart that her husband did the appropriate thing. 'He brought me here to inform my parents, which shows respect toward them. Thank God that he has not decided to leave me in my parents' house. He is not running away from his responsibility. Anyway, how can I doubt him, knowing what he is!'

Subbamma's mother got to work making some snacks and packed food for their journey, along with some gifts that she could afford to send to her daughter's sister-in-law's family. Kodanda and his brother Krishna spent some time with their maternal uncle. Kodanda never grew close to either his mother's side or the father's side of the extended family, as they moved away from that district. Whenever he visited them, it was only for a short time.

The next morning, Sriramulu started his journey with a mix of hope and apprehension. Even at that age, Kodanda felt responsible and took care of his little brother, making sure that he didn't bother his parents who were preoccupied. He sensed that something important was happening in their lives. They reached Chandrala in Krishna district by the evening.

Sriramulu's sister, Lakshamma, was surprised to see her brother with the family coming at that hour. She thought, 'What is happening? No letter, no message. How come my brother is arriving suddenly? I hope everything is ok.' As they were coming through the wooden gate, she looked at their tired faces and, without any questions, welcomed them, hugging her nephews, and took them inside the house. Her husband, Subbarayadu, too arrived by the time they washed up and settled down. Sriramulu quickly narrated the story of their sudden arrival without much introduction.

He said that he tried his best to set things right, but it did not work. He added, "How can I live there losing everything? I will file a case for my portion of property. I will see what I get. I have come to make a living on my own. I came with a hope that you will advise and help me. I am confident that I made the right decision, and I have nothing left there. You both know that I am not afraid of hard work." This took both the husband and wife by surprise. They had an inkling that all was not well at Modepally, but never expected this. Lakshamma, who knew her brother well, recovered first, smiled and said, "I know you, brother, once you make up your mind, no one can stop you. Let us see what can be done; you can tell us all the details later," and looked at her husband, who also smiled and said, "Now that you are here, we will do something. You all had a long journey. Take a bath and let us have our dinner, and then we can talk." Subbamma thought, "Thank God they are not upset," and looked at her husband who threw a knowing glance at her, which seemed to say, 'see I know what I am doing.'

It took a good ten days to figure out what was to be done. Meanwhile, Sriramulu was helping his brother-in-law in his fields, and Subbamma lent a hand with the household chores. Kodanda was happy playing with his 2 cousins, Venkareswarlu who was the same age as him, and the younger one Bhujanga Rao. One evening, the brother-in-law came in and said, "I met the Zamindar of the village Ganapavaram, which is 4 miles from here. He is looking for someone who could draft the legal documents and run the village school." Looking at Sriramulu, he said, "I know you have excellent writing skills, and your handwriting is impeccable. You would be an asset to the villagers. Tomorrow we will go and meet the Zamindar."

The following day, Sriramulu completed his daily tasks and prepared himself ahead of his brother-in-law. They departed together for Ganapavaram, a village close by, where they were warmly greeted by the Zamindar. Observing Sriramulu and conversing with him, the Zamindar felt assured of his ability to assist the villagers in various matters. Expressing a need, he mentioned, "Sir, we lack someone knowledgeable in interpreting the Panchangam to guide us on auspicious and inauspicious days." Such expertise was crucial back then, as people typically commenced important endeavours only when celestial alignments were favourable, a skill possessed only by those well-versed in almanac reading.

Furthermore, he said, "Children in the village are roaming without education, and the school lacks competent teachers. In our sizable village, numerous legal matters remain unaddressed due to a lack of guidance and clerical assistance." He earnestly appealed for Sriramulu's aid, viewing his arrival as an answer to their prayers, a divine intervention.

Sriramulu sensed something genuine in his voice and thought, "I can trust him." He sounds respectful and sincere. 'I hope my gut feeling is right, and I am going to go with it.' He looked at his brother-in-law, who nodded in approval. Zamindar said again, "Please find an auspicious day and come over, we will sort things out." He joined hands in greeting and said, "I will take your leave," and left. Sriramulu and Subbarayadu proceeded toward Chandrala while Subbarayadu started explaining about the village Ganapavaram and Zamindar in detail. After reaching home, they informed the ladies, and Sriramulu said, "I better start working immediately."

His sister smiled, "I know you can't wait. Let us look at the Panchangam (Almanac calendar) for an auspicious day." Looking at him affectionately, she added, "You are on your toes always, relax a bit." Sriramulu said irritably, "What do you know? I have been idling away for almost ten days. Never did I live like this." Lakshamma looked at her sister-in-law, Subbamma, and said, "I wonder how you manage with him." Subbamma smiled and went into the kitchen to get the lunch ready. When they checked the Panchangam, according to Sriramulu's birth star, two days from then turned out to be an auspicious day. His brother-in-law sent a word to the Zamindar that Sriramulu will be starting his work two days hence.

Thus began the most significant journey of Sriramulu's life. It was decided that the family would stay in Chandrala, and he would commute daily. His sister said, "It is hardly four to five miles away. Anyway, it is too soon to set up a home in a new place." Subbamma thought, for how long can I live in my sister-in-law's house? She didn't have the energy to think further, as she was exhausted physically and emotionally. A couple of weeks passed by after by, place full stop and give space Kodanda missed his father who left early in the morning and reached home quite late.

One evening, when everyone sat down to chat after dinner, Sriramulu said, "I don't want to do this commute anymore. The monsoon will be starting soon. Today, Zamindar also said that, and I will not be able to travel back and forth in the rains. He said that there is a vacant house which has all basic amenities, which he will get ready in a day's time. It will be better for me to move there with the family. I think that is the right thing to do. I have looked at the Panchangam; day after tomorrow we will move."

Everyone sensed finality in his voice. His brother-in-law nodded his head and said, "It is true, the monsoon is around the corner. It will get hard to commute daily. Moreover, you must settle down at some point, sooner the better. The boys also should start school." He then got up and said, "I am going to bed," and left.

Lakshamma was not in favour, but she knew that once her brother mad up his mind, even the Gods couldn't reverse it. She said, "Anyway, you will do what comes to your mind, no point talking about it." She, too, got up and went inside.

Subbamma was relieved and happy that she was going to have her own household and thanked her husband silently. On the other hand, she was worried that her sister-in-law would be annoyed. She was the only family around in this far-off land and helped them unconditionally. She thought, 'I will be ever grateful to my sister-in-law and her husband. But how can we live here permanently? We need to move on and live our own lives.' Her husband looked at her and said, "We have to do what we have to. I am going to sleep."

The next day, Subbamma attended to her household chores as usual. Her sister-in-law didn't say much to her. She tried to pacify her sister-in-law by doing more work, but she got sparse responses in monosyllables. Sriramulu did not go to Ganapavaram that day. Kodanda was happy to see his father home when he woke up and asked him, "Nanna, you didn't go today?"

Sriramulu called both his sons and, placing the little one on his lap, cuddling Kodanda, said, "Tomorrow we will be moving to the village Ganapavaram where I have been going all these days. We will have our own home there and settle down. I will be teaching in the school and helping the villagers with their legal matters. You both can study in the school I teach. You have been wasting so much time without proper education. You have to work hard and study well so you can become worthy of yourselves."

Kodanda, quiet as always, nodded his head, but Krishna, the active one, said, "Yes, father, we will. You wait and see; I will study better than my brother. Once I grow up, I will fight with my uncles and bring all our property back. My brother is too soft; he can't fight." Their father laughed and put him down, saying, "You! You are not even as big as my little finger; you talk too much." Both father and Kodanda smiled.

Kodanda, being more mature, started visualizing the new place. "How would it be to go to the school where my father will be teaching?" He wondered how his mother would manage without knowing anyone. "Would she not be lonely? Here, at least, she is with her sister-in-law." Thinking this, he approached his mother and asked her, "Amma, are you happy that we are going to Ganapavaram? Won't you feel lonely?" The mother hugged her son lovingly and said, "Nayana, you are thinking about me! I am really happy that we are going to have our own household. How long can we stay in somebody's house? Traditionally, we are not supposed to live with your father's younger sister. Don't worry about me being lonely, I can make friends; there will be neighbours. There is a saying that 'if your words are sweet, you can win the world.' Teasingly, she said, "Wait and see how many friends your mother will make. Now, go play with your cousins; you will be missing them."

Sriramulu tried to spend some time with his sister, drawing her into conversation about their village, Modepally. He narrated what had been happening regarding their property, which was her favourite topic. By nightfall, she relaxed a bit and called Subbamma and said, "Come now, let us pack some essential things so that you can take with you." She gathered a few utensils and some essential groceries. As she was packing, her brother came in, saw this, and said, "Why are you packing all these things? We can buy once we settle in and you can see what we need." This triggered all the pent-up frustration of Lakshamma, and she exploded saying, "How come you think you know everything? Do you need to interfere in all we do? Can't you leave women's work stuff for us to handle? You are not the one who is going to cook and keep the household running, so keep quiet and leave." Sriramulu guessed the real reason for her anger and said, "Ok, Ok, do whatever pleases you, my mistake," and walked away smiling.

The next morning, they set off before the crack of dawn as it was an auspicious hour. Subbarayudu organized a bullock cart for their journey. Kodanda's cousins were sad when they were leaving. Venkateswarlu, who was closer to Kodanda's age, said, "Amma, why can't I go with Mamayya and Kodanda? I can live with them and go to school there itself." To pacify him, Lakshamma said, "Ok, you can go later but let them settle in first." Venkateswarlu was not happy, started grumbling, but one grunt from his father seemed to settle him down.

As they boarded the bullock cart, Subbamma glanced back at her sister-in-law's house, feeling a mixture of gratitude and sadness. She whispered a silent prayer for her sister-in-law's happiness and well-being. The journey to Ganapavaram was filled with anticipation, new hopes, and unknown apprehensions. Subbamma wondered what their new life would be like in the village, and she hoped they would find acceptance and prosper.

When they reached the village quite early in the morning, the village was just waking up. Subbamma said, "Are we too early? Looks like people are not up yet." As the bullock cart moved slowly further into the heart of the village, they saw a few early risers starting the morning chores. Women were sprinkling cow dung mixed with water in front of their houses and adorning their front yards with muggulu, designs drawn with lime powder in front of houses first thing in the morning. This was supposed to be a good luck charm for the whole day. The men were either milking the cows or getting the bulls ready to go to the fields. They saw some well-to-do farmers ordering their farm helpers around while brushing their teeth with neem sticks. Some of them noticed new faces, stopped what they were doing, and inquisitively looked at them. In a village, everyone knows everyone, including the relatives and friends of the fellow villagers. It is very rare that total strangers would arrive without anyone from the village accompanying them. As they moved further, a few men recognized Sriramulu, whom they saw with the Zamindar. They informed others, saying, "He is Sriramulu; he has been invited by our Zamindar to help us write legal documents and also teach our children in the school."

Everyone's face lit up. They thought, "Finally, we are going to have someone to teach our children." Their stance became friendly, and more welcoming smiles appeared.

A couple of menfolk came forward and said, "Please come, the Zamindar is expecting you, and he made all preparations for your arrival last evening." Meanwhile, a person who worked for Zamindar came on a bicycle, approaching them, and said, "Zamindar sir has sent me. Let me direct you to the house." Soon they reached the house. The front yard had been swept and decorated with lime powder. Subbamma felt that this was an auspicious sign." They noticed two gunny bags and a couple of baskets with some fruits and vegetables in the front veranda. Zamindar's worker came closer and said, "Zamindar sir will come soon. He asked me to tell you that some essential things are in those gunny bags. You can open them, set up everything. If you need anything, please let me know. I will be waiting outside. I will go and bring milk and curd," and left without waiting for an answer. He was back within no time and addressing Subbamma said, "Amma, milk and curd are here, sugar will be in one of the bags. You may be tired after the journey, please have some milk.

Sriramulu looked at his wife and noticed that her eyes were wet with tears. He smiled and said, with a pinch of sadness in his voice, "We have come to the right place. As long as the Zamindar is there, we have nothing to worry about. From the time I met him, he has shown a lot of respect and trust. As long as I work hard and be sincere, we can live here with dignity. Our boys will grow up here, and this is our home now."

Subbamma nodded her head with a quiet smile. Her heart throbbed, hearing the sadness in his voice. He left everything and came here; a man who helped many is now seeking help. She thought, 'My husband's personality is such that he commands respect from everyone. His clean heart reflects in his face, and people are drawn to him.'

As they stepped into the house, they found themselves in 2 small rooms and a kitchen. Kodanda couldn't help but recall their home in Modepally, with its spacious verandas at the front and back, and the expansive backyard. His heart felt a pang of sadness as he reminisced about his uncle, their home, and the vast fields where he spent his days playing. He wondered whether he would ever have the opportunity to return there.

He adored and looked up to his father. Kodanda remembered hearing his parents say time and again that our elder one is an obedient son. The little one is the naughty one. He smiled to himself and thought, "I have to help my parents. I have to study well and make my parents happy, and never trouble them."

Subbamma looked at her son, smiled, and said, "Nayana, all good, we will be fine. Now, come and help me to unpack this stuff." Kodanda, opening one of the gunny bags, thought, My parents seem to be happy. He felt that it looks like we will be living here from now on. Soon, the Zamindar arrived. Sriramulu introduced his family to him. He said to Subbamma, "Amma, please feel at home. We are here if you need anything. Our ladies will come to meet you soon." Then he looked at Kodanda, "Abbayi, you will find friends here soon," and looking at Sriramulu, he said, "Ayya, rest and settle down now. We will meet at the Diwanam later (a mini palace where small Zamindars lived) tomorrow and discuss everything," and left.

Subbamma, while unpacking the bags, thought whether it was appropriate to receive all these things so soon after their arrival. "We brought some basics with us, and we could manage for the time being," she said to her husband. He was a bit annoyed, "You don't have to think that way. I am going to work for every bit I receive, this is in advance for the work that I will do."

Sriramulu wasted no time in immersing himself in his new responsibilities. He began teaching at the school and assisting the villagers with their legal matters. Kodanda and his younger brother, Krishna, started attending the school where their father taught.

Days turned into weeks, and weeks into months. Subbamma gradually found her place in the village, forging friendships with the other women and becoming involved in community activities. She felt a sense of belonging that she had never experienced before.

Sriramulu's dedication to his work and his integrity earned him respect and trust among the villagers. Subbamma's kindness and hospitality made her much beloved among the womenfolk. Her storytelling and singing skills became legendary in the village. People would gather around her to listen to her tales from the epics, Ramayana, and Mahabharatha. She became a source of inspiration and comfort to many. Despite the modest income they earned, Subbamma always ensured that their home was open to anyone in need. Her generosity and resourcefulness endeared her to the villagers even more. Together, they created a home filled with love and generosity.

As the seasons changed and time passed, the family thrived in Ganapavaram. They faced hardships and obstacles along the way, but their bond as a family and their resilience carried them through. Through their hard work, kindness, and unwavering spirit, Sriramulu, Subbamma, and the boys became an integral part of Ganapavaram.

Kodanda, an attentive observer, assumed responsibilities early on. He helped with daily chores, cultivated vegetables, and accompanied his father to school. Rarely did he socialize with other children. He focused on his studies and shared school updates with his mother. He played with his brother and Surayya, a boy next door.

Money was scarce, which was common in villages at that time. Sriramulu was paid for his services by the villagers through various forms of farm produce. The area of Ganapavaram was full of mango groves and paddy fields. There was no dearth of food. Subbamma always prepared extra food, just in in case there were to be sudden visitor, she would have enough to feed them. She would never refuse anyone, especially when it came to food. She would improvise quickly and give them something to eat, and never sent anyone away empty-handed. She would make huge jars of mango and lime pickles, and the villagers knew that if they didn't have anything at home, they could always get some pickle or a curry from Subbamma, when they needed it urgently. As time passed, the womenfolk trusted her and would reach out to seek her advice on various issues. She knew many proverbs and would instantly come up with an appropriate proverb suitable for the situation. People admired her for her spontaneous nature and reciprocity towards her fellow beings.

Sriramulu would often have to visit his native village, Modepally, and at times travel to Guntur to attend the court hearings as the property issue went to court. Subbamma was never happy about the situation. She would feel that all the efforts her husband was making to get either money or property back were futile. Perhaps the money spent on making these trips would also not be recovered, she pondered. Whenever she expressed her displeasure, her husband would get into a fit of anger, and promptly retort, "I let everything go, all we owned has gone to the dogs. Let me salvage whatever I can, what is your problem?"

This episode would happen from time to time. Of course, they never received any substantial funds. Once the court case was settled, Sriramulu never set foot in Modepally again. Kodanda, who had been witnessing all this, somehow developed a kind of detachment and dislike toward Modepally. He, too, never had any interest or inclination to visit Modepally even after he grew up. Both father and son put all this behind them and never looked back.

Sriramulu was busy with the school, helping the villagers, and writing legal documents for the Zamindar, advising people on various issues. Sriramulu's sister and brother-in-law's family also would visit them often. Somehow, Kodanda's cousin, who wanted to come and live with them, never materialized. Whenever Kodanda's aunt came, she would criticize her sister-in-law or complain to her brother, and Sriramulu would yell at his wife. Kodanda loved his aunt, who adored him, but he often was very upset, thinking, "Whenever aunt comes, my mom gets into trouble. Wonder why father always takes her side and reprimands my mother." He could not do much except to help her a bit more with her chores or to say to his mother, "Why is this woman such a troublemaker," to try pacifying his mother. Subbamma would smile and say, "Well, that is her nature, you don't worry, she is older than I, it is ok." Kodanda thought, 'Yes, one respects elders no matter what.'

One day, Krishna got a fever, with cough and cold. Subbamma tried all home remedies without any result, and then they called the local Ayurveda doctor. He came and gave some medicine and said, "This is just a regular fever; he will be okay after taking 3 doses of this medicine," and left. That night, the fever increased, the boy went into delirium, and passed away in Sriramulu's arms.

Subbamma was uncontrollable. It was a shock for Kodanda. He could not see his mother's agony. She cried, saying, "We left everyone and everything that we thought were ours, my Kodanda has become alone. I thought both brothers would grow up together and be there for each other. Why is God testing us this way?" Kodanda never left his mother's side. The whole village was there, consoling Subbamma. Sriramulu busied himself in his work. In time, they found a way to cope with the loss.

Around this time, Sriramulu's family was introduced to Kanakamma, a distant relative of Subbarayudu. She went on a pilgrimage to Kasi with her aged mother when Sriramulu arrived in Ganapavaram, so had not meet earlier. She was widowed at a very young age and had no children of her own. She owned a good amount of land, whose income from the produce she could enjoy, but had no other right to the property according to prevailing law of the time. Only her husband's brothers and their sons would inherit the property after her demise. Subbarayudu took Sriramulu and Subbamma to her house and told her how Sriramulu arrived in Ganapavaram and asked Sriramulu to assist her if needed. Sriramulu, of course, with his big heart and helping nature, took upon himself the responsibility of taking care of both the elderly women.

Both Subbamma and Sriramulu felt very happy that they found some elders they could turn to and were happy to serve them. Sriramulu addressed her as Akkayya (elder sister), and Subbamma called her Vadina (sister-in-law). Sriramulu would find time to enquire after them every day, and Subbamma, too, would often go there to help. As Kanakamma never had anyone she could call her own, she instantly took to this family. She treated Sriramulu as her own brother. Kodanda became the centre of everyone's affection. It is perhaps from such experiences that Kodanda learned from his parents a way to help those in need as one's own.

In a year's time, the couple were blessed with a daughter, Venkayamma, and a couple of years later, a second daughter, Sita, was also born, bringing great joy to the family. Kodanda, who is much older than his sisters, assumed a guardian's role rather than that of a teasing brother. Subbamma's parents came to visit them once and felt happy seeing what their daughter and son-in-law had made of their life. As days passed by, the family felt settled.

Kanakamma's mother passed away, and Sriramulu stood rock solid, performing all the last rites. Kanakamma was overwhelmed, saying, "Which janma's (life) debt are you relinquishing? How many lives do I have to take in order to pay back this debt?" Sriramulu brushed it off, saying, "Akkayya, no need for this kind of talk. We are human beings doing our bit, now stop thinking about all this."

Whatever produce she got from her lands, Kanakamma would share with Sriramulu's family. A sense of belonging grew between them. As Kanakamma was aging, Sriramulu and Subbamma urged her to come and live with them, but she wanted to visit Kasi Viswanath one more time before she got too old to travel. It was getting difficult for Subbamma to finish all her household chores and then go to Kanakamma's house to help her. Kanakamma noticed this and said, "Subbamma, soon we will do something so you don't have to struggle."

Kodanda also felt that his mother was working too hard and tried to help her more. Soon enough, Kanakamma went on her pilgrimage, and when she was back safely, Sriramulu let out a sigh of relief. Those days, traveling to Kasi was not an easy task for people, and to come back from the pilgrimage; it was almost considered a rebirth.

Life, however, never goes without its ups and downs. Almost as if to prove this, something totally unexpected happened. There was a theft in Sriramulu's house. Everything they had – clothes, utensils, some cash that they saved, gifts Subbamma's parents gave, including children's clothes – were stolen. The whole village was in shock. How did this happen? We have let them down. They all thought we are responsible for the safety of this family. Subbamma thought, "It wasn't that long that I was thanking God that we are settled now, and life is going well. I seem to have cast a black eye on my own life."

More than for the loss of her possessions, she suffered from a sense of violation and felt let down. Sriramulu, the practical and worldly-wise man that he was, said, "There will be people who do not like outsiders settling in and garnering so much love and respect. This is life, and we have to deal with it." The whole village, including the Zamindar, came to commiserate with them. He said to Subbamma, "Amma, we are all here; we will catch the thieves. Don't worry." Sriramulu said, "This is how it has to happen; nothing is in our hands. Even if the thieves are caught, we cannot have the things back and use them again. Let it be. I have an inkling as to who it could be. Please let it go."

Zamindar also did not insist on knowing who it is as he too felt that this might be one of those things best left alone. By the next morning, Zamindar and other villagers brought so many things that it surprised the family. Subbamma got more sarees than she had before. There were kitchen utensils, clothes for Sriramulu and children. Like a miracle, the front veranda was filled with bags of grains and other household things needed. The family was moved by the love and affection showered upon them. A keen observer, Kodanda was learning his life lessons.

Sriramulu again began to insist that Kanakamma should come to live with them. Kanakamma called Sriramulu and Subbamma and said, "Nayana, I have some cash. I pledged at the shrine of Kasi Viswanath that you are my brother and that I want to help you to build a house. Please take this cash, buy a piece of land, and build a house. Your family is growing; you need a place of your own. Whatever you are earning is enough to make ends meet. Now that I will also come to live with you, you need a place big enough for all of us. I have no right on the property. I cannot give it in charity, nor can I sell it. If I could, I would adorn my Subbamma with golden jewels from head to foot. I am helpless, I can't give you much." Her eyes filled with tears as she concluded, saying, "I must have done some punya in my previous life, so God sent you to me."

Sriramulu and Subbamma were shocked to hear this. Immediately, Sriramulu said, "Akkayya, we came here leaving all our family behind, and we found everything we lost in you. Your affection is what we are looking for, not any material gains."

Subbamma, tears in her eyes, nodded her head in agreement with her husband. Kanakamma said, "Nayana, don't I know that. Please don't misunderstand me. To whom else will I give whatever I have? You are not only my brother given by God, but a son too who I could never have, in whose hands I will leave this mortal body. Let us not talk more about this and look for a piece of land."

Soon, Sriramulu found a good piece of land. The village well was just adjacent to the land, and the main road was close too. Sriramulu built his house and made Ganapavaram his permanent home. Subbamma later told her grandchildren how their grandfather built the house. He loaded a hundred cartloads of bricks and brought them to the construction site himself from the kiln. With the help of a few workers, he laid the foundation and built their home. The family, along with Kanakamma, moved into the new house. With Kanakamma's help, they bought a couple of buffaloes and planted all kinds of vegetables and flower plants. Kodanda instantly took to gardening. Both mother and son spent a lot of time among the plants. Soon, they also bought one acre of land where they could grow paddy.

Kodanda, watching all this, admired both his parents, working so relentlessly and happily without complaining. He noticed that they enjoyed whatever work they did. He often heard his father saying to his wife, "You forget your husband and children if there is work." While she thought, 'My husband does not know what laziness is.'

Chapter 3
LAYING THE FOUNDATION

Kodanda completed his primary education. Through all the challenges of life, Sriramulu's never lost sight of his son's education. He had to send his son for further studies wherever it was available. Sriramulu had no doubt in his mind about this. Kodanda had to go to Mylavaram, a small town 5 miles from Ganapavaram, to study 1st form (sixth class). Subbamma was worried and sad to send her son away, but she too wanted her son to study.

Sriramulu went to Mylavaram to inquire about schools and accommodation for his son. He went to the only middle school there and approached the headmaster, introducing himself as a document writer and also a teacher who is running a primary school at Ganapavaram. The headmaster said, "Sir, I have heard about you from your village folk. They all have a lot of respect for you and amma. Don't worry about your son; we will admit him to the school. I will have to test him to see his knowledge and accordingly admit him to the suitable class."

Sriramulu said that his son has completed class 5 and should be admitted to the 1st form, (class 6), and added that he is good at his studies. The headmaster smiled and said, "I am sure he will be fine; you must have been teaching him."

Sriramulu said, "I have one more request. I am also looking for some accommodation for the boy; it is not possible for him to commute every day while attending the school. Ganapavaram is 5 miles from here." The headmaster instantly said, "That is not an issue. He can stay in my house. There are a couple of children who also come from other villages who are with us. In our school, we also have other teachers who provide accommodation for children coming from outside. We can organize that. As teachers, if we don't help the students, who will?"

Saying this, he smiled and got up to leave. Sriramulu folded his hands in reverence and said, "Ayya, I cannot forget your help. He is my only son. I hope he studies well and makes something of himself."

The headmaster said, "Of course, it is understandable, the only way for our families to come up in life is through the education of our children. We all need to help each other in this endeavour." Sriramulu thanked him and headed home.

Sriramulu returned home triumphant. He informed Kodanda and Subbamma that everything was arranged settled, and that Kodanda would leave for Mylavaram in two weeks' time. Kodanda had many questions; he waited for his father to rest before asking.

Subbamma immediately began preparing for Kodanda's departure, thinking about all that she needed to get ready for her son. Sriramulu, understanding her thoughts, suggested preparing some snacks and pickles as a small contribution for the teachers who would be helping the students, along with organizing some rice and dal.

That night, after dinner, Kodanda approached his father with his queries, and Sriramulu lovingly cleared all his doubts, assuring him that he would visit him every day, encouraging him to focus on his education.

Kodanda and his father went to Chandrala to inform his aunt and uncle and take their blessings. Lakshamma's first reaction was, "Why are you sending him away to be alone? Is your teaching not enough? What do you want him to be? When you mentioned the last time I met you, I did not think you were serious. Do you want him to become a scholar, your only son? How can you send him away?"

Sriramulu quietly listened to her outburst. Then he said, "Lakshamma, what can I give my son except an education? That is the only way that he can stand up on his feet and take care of the family. I have lost everything. What else can I do?"

This immediately calmed her down, and she felt bad for her hastiness. In her heart, she thought, "I am upset that my son is not interested in studies. He loiters around without a proper education; it is my frustration that I am expressing. This is my nephew whom I love dearly. My son, who has abundant property, has no inclination to study."

Immediately, she said to Kodanda, "Nanna, study well and bring a good name to your father." Looking at Venkateswarlu, she said, "See, he is younger than you, and he is going away to join 1st form. And you are just loitering around."

Venkateswarlu immediately said, "I know, I know, I can never be like your favourite nephew." He got up, took Kodanda by the hand, and walked out to spend some time with his cousin. Both cousins loved each other dearly, despite their mother's occasional taunts.

Sriramulu said, "Lakshamma, if your son goes away, who is going to take care of your lands? Not everybody does the same thing. Don't belittle him in front of everyone. He is a good boy."

The day of departure arrived, and Subbamma prepared special dishes for Kodanda. Sriramulu, following his principles of punctuality and diligence, ensured that they were ready to leave before the scheduled time. Kodanda, receiving blessings from his family and villagers, embarked on his new journey to Mylavaram, leaving home at the age of 12.

Upon reaching Mylavaram, they met the headmaster who warmly welcomed them. Sriramulu expressed his gratitude and concern for his son's well-being, while Kodanda, despite feeling nervous, showed confidence and respect.

"The headmaster called one of the students who was looking curiously at the newcomers and asked him to bring some water to drink. Looking at Kodanda, he said, "So this is the boy," then he looked at Kodanda searchingly and asked, 'What is your name?'

"Kodandaramayya," came the quick answer. He then asked, 'do you know what your name means?'

Kodanda, despite being a quiet child, answered with great confidence, 'Kodandam is the bow of Srirama. As he holds Kodandam in his hand, he acquired the name Kodanda Rama. My father named me after the Kodanda Rama Swamy of Tirupathi.'

Sriramulu noticed a smile on the headmaster's face and thought, 'My son has won his heart; he will be fine now.' The headmaster said, 'You not only know the meaning but also know how you got the name. Good. Are you ready to stay here, away from your parents, and study?'

Kodanda nodded his head. The headmaster noticed some sadness on his face. Cheering him up, he said, "There are other students here away from their families; you will make friends with them. If you concentrate on your studies, time will go by quickly." Turning toward the boys standing there, who seemed to be of the same age as Kodanda, he introduced them and asked them to take Kodanda inside to show him where he can keep his bag.

Sriramulu opened the bags and handed over the things he had brought. The headmaster said, "Why did you take so much trouble carrying all this while you came on foot?" Then he summoned one of the boys to take them inside. Kodanda suddenly remembered his mother saying that she packed some snacks separately for him. Now, father gave the whole thing to them. Of course, he could not say anything, except to think that "My father never pays attention to whatever mother says." Meanwhile, the headmaster's wife came out and saw Kodanda, looked at the headmaster, and said, 'Oh, is this the new boy you were mentioning?' She then looked at Kodanda, smiled, and said, 'Good looking boy, seems intelligent too.'

The headmaster smiled, 'Let us see.' Sriramulu said to her, "Amma, this is my only son. I have two daughters younger to him. This is the first time he will be away from home. My wife and I will be ever grateful to you."

She said, "Please don't worry. I understand your concern. These children leave their parents and come to pursue their future. We love and care for them like our own." Sriramulu took out some money and gave it to the headmaster toward the school fees. He said, "Ayya, when I come next time, I will arrange to give you some money toward his stay."

The headmaster looked at Sriramulu and said, "You have to pay the school fees. I cannot help you there. Don't worry much about paying me for room and board. If the child studies well and comes up, we will be happy." Sriramulu thought, "What a generous person he is!" Whenever Sriramulu came to visit, he always brought food stuff from his farm and also gave some amount he could afford. Sriramulu thanked him once more and walked toward his son, saying, 'Nayana, I will be leaving now. Be an obedient student, serve your teacher, be friendly with the other students. Study well. I will come again and see you.'" Then he looked at the headmaster and said, 'If I go now, I can reach home before it gets dark. I would like to take your leave.'

The headmaster's wife said, "Let me give you some buttermilk; it will be tiresome walking back all the way." She went in and came back with a big glass of buttermilk.

Sriramulu drank it and felt refreshed. Kodanda did not utter a word. Sriramulu hugged his son one more time and walked away without looking back.

As promised, he used to walk all the way to Mylavaram every day to see his son and bring him some food. The headmaster noticed this and said one day, "Sir, why are you doing this, walking such a long distance every day? We are here looking after your son. Trust us, he will be fine. Come on Friday evening to take him home. Don't tire yourself unnecessarily."

Hearing this, Sriramulu looked at his son. Kodanda said, "Nanna that is true. I am fine. Please don't come every day. I will come home on the weekend anyway. You will get tired, and your work too will be affected." Sriramulu smiled and said, "All right, you are a grown boy who can stay on your own and study. Let it be. I will come on Friday to pick you up. Study hard and listen to the teacher, do whatever he asks you to do."

The headmaster said, "You don't worry about that. He is an obedient child." An interesting incident that happened which shows the courageous side of his character. Once when a teacher in the class called out loudly, "Silence, silence, don't make noise," Kodanda said, "Sir, your noise is more than our noise." The teacher got wild and boxed his ears red. When Sriramulu came to know about this, he said, "Nayana, you are not supposed to say this to your teacher. You must apologize to him," even though his heart ached for his dear son.

Kodanda, along with three other students, lived at the headmaster's house. He would wake up at five in the morning, after brushing with a neem stick, and fill water in the big cement tubs from the well. Then he would take a bath and go to the nearby freshwater well and bring 3 or 4 pots of water for cooking and drinking needs of the whole family. He would then change his clothes and study until the master's wife called them for the morning meal, which consisted of rice, pickle, and buttermilk. Along with the other boys, he would walk to school and come back for lunch. In the evening, they would get some dry snacks and dinner at 7 o'clock, Vegetable, Charu (a kind of soup), and buttermilk along with rice.

Kodanda had a strong sense to discerning right from wrong. He was an above-average student, as far as the marks were concerned, but beyond mere academic performance, what marked him was a deep quest for knowledge. He respected and followed rules and was an obedient student who never hesitated to speak his mind when something unfair happened. He grew up a friendly introvert. The unconditional love he got from his family, especially from his parents, meant he didn't feel the need for any other emotional support from outside, and this gave him a lot of self-confidence.

Whenever he was helping his teacher or his wife with household chores, it was always heartfelt, and he worked with sincerity and reverence. Somehow, his work stood apart from other children, and the elders noticed this and silently appreciated it.

At home, Kanakamma passed away. The family felt the loss deeply. While she was alive, they felt secure, knowing they had an elderly person to turn to in times of need, and for moral support. Sriramulu performed all the last rites with a lot of reverence. After all the ceremonies were done, Kanakamma's relatives came and took all her property documents, marking the end of Sriramulu's connection with her. All they were left with were her memories.

A couple of years passed since Kodanda joined the school in Mylavaram. He completed the first and second form schooling (sixth and seventh classes) and had one more year in Mylavaram to complete the third form. He would then have to move to Vijayawada for the 4th form (9th class), which is high school. Sriramulu went to Mylavaram to bring his son home for summer holidays. They went to take leave from the headmaster. He blessed Kodanda and said, "You did well, Nayana. You have a good future." The headmaster turned to Sriramulu and said, "Sir, my wife is a bit unwell; it is getting difficult for her to tend to all these boys. It will be helpful if you can find another place for Kodanda to stay from next year. I also have to inform the other boys. Now that we have summer holidays, you will have enough time to arrange for his stay." Sriramulu immediately said, "Surely, sir, I will look into it. You have been so helpful; I will not burden amma. You have kindly taken care of him when he had to stay away from home for the first time. Now he can stay anywhere without much difficulty." Saying so, he took leave and proceeded home. Both father and son, engrossed in their own thoughts, reached home.

Subbamma was happy that her son came home and that he would stay for a while. When Sriramulu informed his wife that they had to look for a different place for the next year, Subbamma said with a sigh, "Problems never stop, where to look for another place?" Sriramulu walked out without saying a word. She thought nothing perturbed him. Taking her son by the hand, she walked inside.

Two days later, Subbarayudu came along with Lakshamma to Ganapavaram. They were happy to see Kodanda. Lakshamma hugged him and said, "My nephew is a grown man now. He stays on his own, away from all of us, and studies," and kissed him on his head.

Sriramulu said, "Yes, but now we have a problem. We have to look for another place this year. He can't stay in the headmaster's house anymore, as his wife is unwell." Immediately, Subbarayudu said, "I'm acquainted with a family in Mylavaram. The man is a teacher at the same school as the headmaster. They don't have children of their own; his widowed sister-in-law lives with them. I'll write a letter for you to give to them. It would be nice for them as well to have Kodanda live with them."

Subbamma felt relieved. Sriramulu looked at her with a mocking smile and said, 'See, problems do get solved; there is no point worrying unnecessarily.' Subbarayadu got up to leave and tripped as he tried to walk. Sriramulu hurried to him, holding his arm, and said, "Bava, are you alright? What happened?"

Lakshamma said, "He has been feeling unwell for the last couple of days. He gets dizzy but is refusing to see the doctor. He says, "I will be fine. I will wait for a couple of days, and if it still persists, then go." What can I do? Maybe you should come take him. Can you come in a couple of days after settling Kodanda in?" Sriramulu said, "Of course, I will be there. Day after tomorrow, I will go to Mylavaram, settle Kodanda's stay, and come."

Sriramulu and Kodanda walked them to the end of the village, assuring his sister that he would come to her soon. Sriramulu went to Mylavaram two days later with Kodanda and met the family recommended by his brother-in-law. They were more than happy to take Kodanda into their house. The teacher said, "I know the headmaster well. Tell him that you are coming to stay with me. He is a good man. We have to help him as his wife is not well." He also inquired about Subbarayudu and his welfare, mentioning that he too hails from Chandrala but his father moved to Mylavaram." Sriramulu thanked him, "We will be back as soon as the school reopens after the holidays."

Happy that everything was settled, both father and son headed home. By the time they reached home, it was quite dark. They saw Subbamma and the girls waiting for them with a worried look. Sriramulu smiled and said, "All is well. They are nice people. Kodanda is fine. Now, let us have dinner soon and go to bed. I have to leave for Chandrala in the morning to take my brother-in-law to the doctor."

With a sigh of relief, everyone went into the house to have their dinner. After dinner, Subbamma said, "You had a hectic day today. Why don't you go the day after to Chandrala?" As she was saying this, she knew that her husband would not heed her advice. Once he makes up his mind, he will do exactly what he wants. Sure enough, he said, "I waited just to settle Kodanda. I should have gone earlier. It is important to take my brother-in-law to the doctor soon."

Sriramulu headed to Chandrala early in the morning. Midway, he saw Subbarayudu coming towards Ganapavaram. Sriramulu said, "Bava, what are you doing here? I am coming to take you to the doctor." Subbarayudu smiled and said, "I am fine. Your sister unnecessarily makes a fuss. I have some work in Ganapavaram. The Zamindar is disposing of some property which belongs to him in Chandrala. He wanted to consult me and requested me to come. Let us go back." Sriramulu looked at his brother-in-law's face searchingly and said, "Bava, are you sure? What do we lose if we check with the doctor once?" Subbarayudu said, "Now, you don't follow your sister. I am fine." He started walking fast as though to prove to Sriramulu that he is fine. As they reached the village, he said, "Tell Subbamma that I will come for lunch after I finish my work," and went away. Sriramulu went back home.

The family was enjoying themselves, with Kodanda being at home. Sriramulu got back to his busy schedule, and Subbamma spent a lot of time with her son. A couple of days had passed since Subbarayudu's visit. One night, after the family had gone to bed, Subbamma heard a knock at the door. Without waking up Sriramulu, she wondered who could be there at such an unearthly hour, and went to the door asking, "Who is it?" She heard a voice, "Amma, I am coming from Chandrala. Lakshamma sent me to bring Ayya garu. Subbarayudu ayya is unwell." Subbamma opened the door and asked the messenger to wait. She tried to wake up Sriramulu. Normally a light sleeper, Sriramulu took a bit of time to wake up. He looked at his wife. "What is going on? What is the time? Why are you waking me up at this time?" Subbamma said, "Nothing serious, only that a messenger came from Chandrala. He says that your brother-in-law is not too well."

Hearing this, Sriramulu got up immediately, went out, and seeing his brother-in-law's farm helper said, "Rangayya, what happened?" He replied, saying, "Babu, Ayya is not well. Amma wants me to bring you. I don't know more than that." Sriramulu said, "What do you mean by saying I don't know more?" He quickly went in. While dressing himself up, he called to his wife and said, "I am going now. I will send word in the morning as to how things are. If needed, you can come."

Without waiting for Subbamma's response, he walked out. Subbamma was worried. She thought, 'I should have gone too. Kodanda is home; the girls will not be alone. This man has no patience; he left without even discussing the matter. I would have been of some help to my sister-in-law. Why did he have to rush without waiting? Hope Annayya is okay.' With such thoughts racing through her mind, she could not get back to sleep. After a couple of hours, she got up and started her morning chores.

Usually, Sriramulu would fill water into the 2 big cement tubs in front and back of the house from the well for household usage. Subbamma would bring a couple of pots of water from the drinking water well, which was some distance from their home. She would bathe at the well and bring water for drinking and cooking. Food was offered to God every day before they ate. This is an age-old custom in many households. They never miss this, even in dire circumstances.

That day, Subbamma, unable to sleep, went to the well while it was still dark to draw water to fill the tubs herself, as Sriramulu was not there to do his usual work. While she was doing so, one of the neighbours who came for water asked, "Amma, what happened? Where is Babayya? Why are you drawing water at this early hour?"

She told him what had happened. Taking the bucket from her hand, he said, "Amma, let me help you with drawing the water.

You hurry and finish the other work soon; who knows what news we have to hear. Even you may have to go." Subbamma reluctantly let the bucket go, saying, "You are right. I will go and try to get some work done," and started her daily chores. Kodanda got up and when he didn't see his father, asked his mother. She explained to him what had happened and said, "Nayana, I may have to go depending on the situation. Now that you are here, take care of your sisters." Absentmindedly, she went on with her work. She finished cooking and fed the children. Kodanda said, "Amma, why don't you eat; who knows when father will come?"

As he was saying this, a bullock cart stopped at the gate, and a man quickly alighted. Kodanda hurried to him. Subbamma, too, walked to the gate and recognized Rangayya and said, "What happened, Rangayya?" With tears in his eyes, Rangayya said, "Amma, Sriamulu Garu has asked me to bring you all" (meaning Sriramulu), "Our Ayya passed away." Subbamma sat down and said, "How is it possible? Barely two days ago, he was here having lunch. I can't believe this."

Kodanda quickly came to his mother and, holding her hand, said, "Amma, get up, let us go fast. Nanna and Attayya must be waiting." Subbamma got up slowly, went inside, and stuffed a few clothes in a bag. She told Kodanda to inform the neighbours and get into the cart. Kodanda said, "Amma, you did not eat anything; have something."

Subbamma said, "This is not the time to eat. I should not eat after hearing such news." Kodanda said, "Please have some milk, at least." She quickly arranged everything, locked the house, and as she was getting into the bullock, a few neighbours came and said, "Time has come for him to go, a real gentleman. All of us in Ganapavaram know him and respect him." Subbamma responded with tears in her eyes, "I wonder how my sister-in-law is holding up. Her children are still young; God only knows how she is going to manage."

She requested her neighbours "Keep an eye on the house. I have no idea when we will be back." They all, with one voice, assured her, "That is the last thing you have to worry about. We are here. Go and do what you have to." Subbamma nodded and said, "Ok, Rangayya, let us go now. Hurry up," and waved her hand to the people who came to see her off. Subbamma reached Chandrala and saw that people from the villages around were present there as Subbarayudu was a well-respected gentleman. She went to her sister-in-law and sat down next to her, holding her hand. Lakshamma, seeing her sister-in-law, cried aloud, saying, "Subbamma, your brother left me, leaving all this on my head."

Sriramulu, of course, took up the responsibility and made the necessary arrangements. He stood by his sister and helped her in all respects. Lakshamma, displaying remarkable courage, confronted the challenging circumstances head-on, taking charge of the situation. She actively managed the property, overseeing the cultivation of various crops, and supervising the workers. Despite facing criticism, particularly from her husband's family, she remained resolute. When she overheard disparaging remarks, she boldly responded, emphasizing her responsibility in raising her three sons and a daughter. She asserted her determination not to entrust such matters to others, expressing concerns about potential deceit and the lack of recourse. She invited anyone with objections to confront her directly, affirming that she was not doing anything unethical.

After that, no one dared to criticize her. She became the talk of the town, and people admired her courage for a long time. Kodanda loved his aunt and looked up to her. He later mentioned her great courage to many. She took help from her brother only when necessary, saying, 'You have a family to take care of. I will ask you if I need something.'

Kodanda went back to Mylavaram to continue his studies. He quickly adjusted to the new place. The teacher's sister-in-law developed a lot of affection toward Kodanda and treated him with love and care. Once, when Kodanda had a boil on his right hand and couldn't mix his food to eat, she mixed the rice and fed him. Kodanda never forgot this gesture, long after he grew up.

In Ganapavaram, the Zamindar passed away, this was a big blow to Sriramulu. The support from that quarter also stopped. Ganapavaram was also growing. A bus service to Mylavaram and a couple of other villages started. People were able to sell some of their produce in the nearby town. Awareness of the importance of education had also increased. With the bus service, many children started going to other places to study. Earlier, they were content with whatever education they could get in their village and started working afterward. The number of children studying with Sriramulu also slowly diminished.

As the children were growing, expenses were also increasing. Things in the village changed significantly. People who used to give produce from their farms were now not as generous as before, as they started selling their produce to make money. Whatever little help they received from Kanakamma when she was alive, had stopped after her passing.

After finishing the 3rd form, Kodanda had to move from Mylavaram to Vijayawada to join the 4th form. Again, the question of finances cropped up. Sriramulu started thinking about how he was going to figure this out. He never wavered in his conviction to give his son a proper education. His entire his focus was on seeing his son succeed; he was convinced that education was the only means open to him to lead a good life.' He never lingered on past setbacks. Kodanda also inherited his father's optimistic outlook, always moving forward and only reflecting on past errors for learning.

Sriramulu decided to make a trip to Vijayawada and to meet a couple of his acquaintances. When he told Subbamma, she thought, 'Okay, again he is on a mission.' She prayed that he would successfully finish the work. Kodanda thought that maybe he should accompany his father but did not have the courage to ask him, thinking that it would incur more expenses. He thought, 'If father asked, I will go,' but Sriramulu did not ask; he simply said, 'Nayana, I will go arrange everything and take you.' Apart from the fees, the question of his accommodation also needed to be addressed.

Sriramulu had to take a bus to Mylavaram first and then another bus to Vijayawada. By the time he reached, it was around lunchtime. He waited at the bus stand for a while, ate something Subbamma packed, and then went to see a distant relative, Krishnayya, whom he met in Guntur while he was attending to his property cases at the court. Krishnayya was a pleader clerk who worked at the Guntur court. He was also from a Pamidighantam family. If a Pamidighantam family person hears about another Pamidighantam person, the immediate reaction would be, 'He is our Pamidighantam man.' An inexplicable closeness was felt. They felt warmth and an obligation to help each other.

Sriramulu explained the situation about his son's education to him. Krishnayya said, 'I wonder if you know Sriramamurthy, our Pamidighantam man, who was adopted by a well-to-do Kothuri family. He is also a councillor for Vijayawada and runs several businesses. You should approach him. Being a Pamidighantam originally, I heard he does have a soft corner for us. I am sure he will do something for your son.'

Hearing this, Sriramulu took his address and proceeded to Sriramamurthy's house in Vijayawada. He reached Sriramamurthy's house around 3 P.M. As he was about to knock at the door, Sriramamurthy, who was about to go out, opened the door and looked at Sriramulu enquiringly. Sriramulu introduced himself, saying, "I am coming from Ganapavaram. Pamidighantam Krishnayya had asked me to meet you." Sriramamurthy invited Sriramulu into the house and called for someone to bring water. Taking this opportunity, Sriramulu traced their common Pamidighantam family connection from Modepally before Sriramamurthy was adopted. Sriramamurthy said, "Oh, then you will be my elder brother," and smiled fondly. Sriramulu explained that he has come to ask for help regarding his son's education and said that he has to be admitted in the 4th form and also to arrange a stay for him.

Sriramamurthy thought for a while without speaking much. Then he said, "I know the principal of the high school. We can go and talk to him. I will take care of the fees, and the boy can come and dine with us. We will have to think about his stay. I know a teacher who is working in the intermediate college, Ramachandrudu, who has a couple of students stay with him. I will speak to him. Come back in a couple of weeks, and bring your son along. We will admit him to the school, and at the same time, we can talk to Ramachandrudu about his stay. Once everything is settled, you can go and come back after the school reopens."

He called his wife and introduced Sriramulu, explaining the relationship. He then said, 'His son will be coming here to join the fourth form (which is class 9), and I have asked him to have meals with us.' She smiled and nodded, saying, 'Surely, no problem. It is nice to help children who are interested in studying,' and went inside to send some buttermilk for Sriramulu.

Sriramulu immediately said, 'Yes, I will do that,' and thanked Sriramamurthy. Sriramamurthy said, 'Annayya, please don't thank me. We are one family. If I can't do even this, what is the use of being of the same family?' Sriramulu didn't say much but thought, 'That is your generosity. You are a good man.'

Taking his leave Sriramulu departed, saying that he would be back in a couple of days. He reached the bus stop for the return journey, hoping to catch the last bus. He was prepared to have to spend the night in the bus stand, if he missed the last bus. No such thing happened. He got into the bus, which was about to depart, and sighed with relief. By the time he reached home, it was past 10 PM.

At home, the children had their dinner. The girls were half asleep. Kodanda and Subbamma were waiting for Sriramulu, periodically glancing at the main road, which was a couple of hundred yards from their house. As they saw the bus arriving, they held their breath to see if it would stop. To their great relief, the bus stopped, and they noticed in the light of the bus someone getting down. They hoped it was Sriramulu. There were no streetlights then, so they could not see clearly. Kodanda took the kerosene lantern and walked to the gate and a bit beyond. Lifting the lantern, he saw the person walking toward him and thought, 'Ah, it is father,' and walked quickly to reach his father. Sriramulu saw his son, and though tired, his face lit up. He said, 'Nayana, you're still awake! It is so late; why are you not sleeping?'

He placed a hand on his son as they both walked together. Subbamma saw them walking together and smiled, saying, "Thank God, you reached safely. We were wondering whether you would be able to catch the last bus or not."

Sriramulu knew they were waiting for the news. He said with a smile, "All is well. I have to take Kodanda in a couple of days to admit him into school and meet the people where he will stay. I will tell you the details later."

Kodanda said, "Nanna, come and take your bath first, and have your dinner. Amma is also waiting. We can talk later." He went into the backyard to fill the bucket with hot water for his father. As they were eating, Sriramulu told them all the details and then said that it was time to get to bed as it was late, and he went to the veranda where he usually slept. Kodanda stayed with his mother until she cleared up everything after dinner, bolted the back door and went to bed.

Over the next few days, Sriramulu got very busy with some document work, which was his main source of income. Sriramulu and Kodanda left ten days later for Vijayawada by the early morning bus. By the time they reached, it was 10 am. They went straight to Sriramamurthy's house. When they knocked on the door, Sriramamurthy himself opened it. He looked at them and said, "Sriramulu Annayya, come, come, I was wondering about your arrival only. They opened the admissions, and children are being enrolled. Good you are here." He then looked at Kodanda. As soon as Sriramamurthy set eyes on Kodanda, he felt an unknown affection for him.

Their relationship quickly grew. Sriramamurthy said, "Have something to eat, and then we will first go to the school to get the admission work done, and then we can see Ramachandrudu. If it gets late, we will have our lunch and then go." He went inside and told his wife that they would be coming for lunch, but to give the father and son something to eat. His wife, Janakamma, brought some puffed rice with milk and bananas. Sriramulu said, "Amma, we are troubling you." She smiled gently, "Don't mention that. Please have something to eat. You must have left home very early."

Kodanda and Sriramulu left with Sriramamurthy to SKPVVH High School as soon as they were done eating. Kodanda was excited, and of course a bit scared. Sriramamurthy went straight to the principal's office, as he knew him well, and introduced Sriramulu and Kodanda, saying that Sriramulu was himself a teacher and a well-versed document writer.

Getting a place in the school was not difficult in those days. After registration and payment of fees, they thanked the principal and came out. Sriramulu thought that the work was done without much hassle because of Sriramamurthy. Sriramamurthy looked at Kodanda and said, "Do you like the school? Now you have to study well. See how your father is working hard to give you an education."

Kodanda nodded his head and, with great zeal, said, "I will study well." Both Sriramulu and Sriramamurthy smiled. Kodanda was a bit annoyed, thinking, 'I am not a child anymore. I will be 15 soon. I know my responsibility. I must start earning soon and take care of my family.' Thinking thus, he smiled to himself and thought, 'Maybe that is how parents feel about their children. I should not be upset.'

It was around 12 noon. They decided to go to Sriramamurthy's house to have lunch, rest a bit, and then go and see Ramachandrudu, and leave for Ganapavaram from there.

As planned, they reached Ramachandrudu's house by 3 PM. Ramachandrudu opened the door and invited them in, asking them to sit. Sriramamurthy then introduced Sriramulu and Kodanda, saying, "Ramachandra, this is the boy I was telling you about. We got admission at the high school, and everything is set. He will be coming to our place for dinner."

Immediately, Ramachandrudu said, "Yes, yes, I remember." He looked at Kodanda and said, "Looks like a sharp fellow. He can stay with us. I also have another boy who is from Guntur, our distant relative, and a boy from Nuzividu. They will keep each other company."

He stepped inside and asked for some coffee to be served. Sriramulu said, "I don't drink coffee. I will have some water. Thank you very much for housing my son. It is very kind of you." Ramachandrudu nodded and said, "Sriramamurthy is very close to me. Once he recommends, I have no problem. My wife and I will be happy if the boys study well and succeed."

Then, he asked Sriramulu about Ganapavaram and his background. Sriramulu quickly narrated his story. Ramachandrudu smiled and said, "True, that is the dream of every father. Do not worry, your son seems bright. He will do well."

Then he started chatting about various things with Sriramamurthy. As they were chatting, coffee and buttermilk were served for the guests. It seemed like Ramachandrudu was in the mood to chat. Sriramulu was getting a bit restless and wanted to leave. He mentioned a couple of times that he would have to go, but Ramachandrudu didn't take note of it in his enthusiasm of talking with Sriramamurthy. After a while, Sriramamurthy was the one who noticed and said, "I think he should leave now, or he will miss his bus. I too must go; I have some work to attend to. Ramachandra, you are a great talker. You make people forget everything once you start talking."

He laughed and got up to leave. Ramachandrudu also laughed aloud and, turning to Sriramulu, said, "My wife is not here; she has gone to Ongole to visit her sister. You can meet her when you come to drop off your boy after the holidays. Come a day or two before the school reopens. Vijayawada is a big town, and the boy can go around and get to know the place before the school starts." Sriramulu thanked him and said, "I will do that. That is a good idea. Now, I will take my leave."

Kodanda also looked at him and joined his hands, saying namaskaram. They walked for a distance in silence. "Now you take a rickshaw to the bus stand from here. I have to go in the opposite direction." Sriramulu thanked him again for all his help and said, "I will meet you when I come to leave the boy."

They hurried to get a rickshaw to go to the bus stand. When they reached the bus stand, they had ample time to catch the bus. Before getting into the bus, Sriramulu went and bought some bananas and oranges, some for them to eat there, and some to take home. Both father and son did not talk much on their return journey as both got lost in their own thoughts.

When they reached home, it was still twilight. Sriramulu quickly told his wife what had happened and went out to attend to some work as it was still daylight. Kodanda, tired and lost in thought, reluctantly answered his mother's inquiries about the place, school, and the people with whom he was going to stay. Subbamma noticed this and stopped, saying apologetically, "Nanna, go take your bath and rest. We can talk later. I am being so inconsiderate. Without thinking how tired you must be, I kept going with my questions." Kodanda smiled and said, "It is okay, amma. I know you are anxious. After my bath, I will come and tell you everything in detail," and took a towel and went to take his bath.

That night, after Subbamma served dinner to Sriramulu and the kids, and when she sat down to have her meal, Kodanda also sat next to her as usual to keep her company, which he always did whenever he is at home. Mother and son would usually chat away about everything under the sun until Sriramulu would come and say, "When will your chatting ends for you to go to bed? The sun will be up soon." That day Sriramulu did not say anything; he went and slept quietly. Kodanda narrated their journey, talked about Sriramamurthy and Ramachandrudu, and also about the school. Subbamma patiently listened and then said, "Nayana, Vijayawada is so far off; your father cannot come and visit you as often as he used to when you were in Mylavaram. Living with strangers, I am worried about so many things: your food, place of stay, and the kind of people with whom you will be interacting."

She turned her head to the other side so Kodanda would not see her tears. Kodanda felt very bad for his mother and said, "Amma, how can you be so naive? Did I not manage my food and bed in Mylavaram? I can adjust. We need to work hard to achieve something. You yourself say this. See how hard father and you are working. Mylavaram is one bus, and Vijayawada is two buses away. I enjoy bus rides. There is the goddess Kanakadurga temple in Vijayawada. I will run up every day and pray to her, and I will ask her to keep you well. If I study well, your son will be a degree holder."

He tried to make the situation lighter and made his mother laugh. Subbamma pretended to be angry and said, "You have learned to talk like a city-bred clever boy even before going there. Go now, no need to talk to me," and got up to clear her dinner stuff. Laughing, Kodanda said, "Amma, I am your son. Look how you mesmerized Ganapavaram people with your talk, and you have so many admirers. I think I take after you," and he began helping his mother. The mother quietly finished her work, held her son's head, and kissed his head, saying, "Now, enough talk, go and sleep. I am also tired and ready to get some sleep."

Kodanda quietly crept into his father's bed, thinking, 'Amma always kisses on the head whenever she is amused or overwhelmed with affection.' Smiling to himself, he placed his hand on his father and fell asleep immediately.

The summer holidays went by quickly, and it was time for Kodanda to leave for Vijayawada. Kodandaramayya went to Chandrala to take his aunt's blessings and also to meet his cousins. They were all very happy to see him. His aunt said, "Kodanda, you came all alone. Where is your father?" Kodanda said, "He has to attend to some work before we leave for Vijayawada, so I came to see you."

His aunt said, smiling with pride, "I am so glad you came. Now you are a grown man." Kodanda had his lunch there and returned home. As soon as he came home, his mother said, "I was waiting for you. I thought you would come back for lunch. As you are leaving tomorrow, I made your favourite *garelu* (Dal dumplings). You could have them come for lunch?"

She sounded annoyed. Kodanda said, "How did you think that my aunt would let me leave without eating, amma? Come now, please, don't be upset. I am leaving tomorrow."

He went and hugged his mother. Sriramulu, who had just entered, saw this and said, "enough of you both, mother and son drama. Get to work now and start packing."

As usual, Subbamma and Sriramulu packed everything required for Kodanda, some fresh vegetables, and some sweets and savouries for Ramachandrudu. Everything was in order and fully packed the day before the journey. Kodanda felt sad leaving everyone at home. With a heavy heart, he bid farewell to his five and eight-year-old sisters, and to the villagers, who were more in number this time as he was going to Vijayawada. He was one of the first young men leaving the village and going all the way to Vijayawada for higher studies.

Kodandaramayya left Ganapavaram for Vijayawada in 1942 when he was 16 years old. His real journey of life started then. Alone, burdened with the responsibility of the whole family on his shoulders, with meagre monetary support in an unfamiliar land, he was nervous but not afraid. Stepping out of the bus in Vijayawada, Kodandaramayya was apprehensive and wondered about his unknown future. On the other hand, he was also looking forward to facing the adventure in Vijayawada with excitement. This would be the first time that he would be completely alone in a big city. He had to fend for himself in every way. Both the father and son ate the snacks and fruit Subbamma packed for them, then, took a rickshaw to Ramachandrudu's house.

Kodanda looked at the surroundings of Vijayawada with a different perspective this time. He thought, 'This will be home for some time. I am going to live here and spend a lot of time in this town.' He instantly fell in love with the town. Later, too, he used to say Vijayawada was his favourite town.

They reached Ramachandrudu's house. As they walked through the gate, they saw Ramachandrudu sipping his coffee, sitting in the easy chair after finishing his daily puja. He quickly got up from his chair and walked a couple of steps down, welcoming them, saying, "Please come. I was wondering about your arrival, as the school is going to reopen in two days. I am glad you are here. This way, Kodandaramayya can look around and get used to the town."

As Kodanda heard his full name being used as Kodandaramayya, he quickly looked at his father, who smiled and turned toward Ramachandrudu, and greeted him. Kodandaramayya understood that somehow the time has come when he will be called by his full name in this new place. This also reminded him that he is growing up. All his childhood he was addressed as Nayana, Kodanda, or Abbayi, now he had to get used to Kodandaramayya.

Sriramulu quickly unpacked all the stuff they brought and put it on the veranda floor. Ramachandrudu called out to his wife, and when she came out, he introduced Sriramulu and Kodandaramayya saying, "You were in Ongole when they came last time. He is the boy who is going to stay with us. They are related to Sriramamurthy."

She looked at Kodandaramayya, smiled and said, "Yes, yes, I recall you telling me." She asked Kodandaramayya to bring his trunk inside the house and showed him where to place it. Then she looked at him affectionately and said, "All through summer, we sleep in the verandah on a mat. Only in winters, when it gets cold, we all sleep in this hall." Kodanda nodded and said, "No problem, amma. I can sleep anywhere."

She then said, "Let me fix something for you to eat. You must be hungry." Then, Kodandaramayya said, "No, no, we already ate. My mother packed some food, and we are full."

As he walked out, Ramachandrudu was talking to Sriramulu, about how the independence movement is gaining momentum all over the country. They predicted that achieving independence is not far. He said, "I never thought I would live to see a free India. Now, I will also live in freedom and die as a free man, not as a slave to these Britishers."

He also talked at length about people from and around Vijayawada participating in the freedom struggle, and that many are in prisons, and how their families are struggling to make both ends meet. As he was talking, he got very excited and continued saying, "Gandhiji visited Vijayawada and Andhra Pradesh at least four times. His visits inspired the youth as well as women. Many women bravely sent their husbands and children to the prisons". He said, "When Gandhiji was here, he stayed in the house of Golla Narayana Rao, who donated his wife's jewellery worth Rs. 2,500 to Gandhiji toward Swarajyanidhi." He further added, proudly, that he personally knows Narayana Rao.

Sriramulu patiently listened but was not very keen on the conversation. He always lived in a village, taking care of the family, property, and living a pious life as his priority. He was, of course, aware that the country is under British rule, and Gandhiji and others are striving for independence. He knew that we need to get rid of the foreign rule. However, he was not aware of the details and was also not too keen on knowing them.

When Sriramulu saw Kodandaramayya coming out, to end the conversation politely, he said, "Hope we get our independence soon. We will visit Sriramurthy and I will drop the boy here and will proceed to Ganapavaram by the 3 o'clock bus. The women folk are all alone there."

Ramachandrudu somehow realized that he had been going on in his own stride, smiled and said, "Of course, do visit Sriramamurthy, but you must come and have lunch here with Kodandaramayya. He will also feel good. I insist on that."

Sriramulu said, "No need to trouble amma." As he was saying this, Ramachandrudu's wife came out and said, "Annayya, no trouble at all. Please come back for lunch after meeting Sriramamurthy Annayya." Sriramulu could not say anything more. He agreed and said, "Ok, amma. If you insist, I will be back soon," and left for Sriramamurthy's house."

As they arrived, they saw Sriramamurthy entering the house at the same time from the opposite direction. He looked at them, smiled, and said, "Oh, you are here. I was thinking about you this morning and wondered when you would be arriving. Come in."

As they walked in, he again said, "Looks like you have already met Ramachandrudu. How is he?" Sriramulu asked, "He is well. We also met his wife this time; they both seem to be very nice. In fact, they insisted that we go back and have lunch there before I go to Ganapavaram. We came to see you and thank you for everything and for Kodanda to take your blessings," he said, looking at his son fondly. Sriramamurthy said, "Of course, I will look out for him. I don't remember if I mentioned to you earlier, I have become very fond of him. I can see that he will reach great heights."

He looked at Kodandaramayya and placed his hand affectionately on him, smiling. They went inside, sat for a bit, and Sriramulu said, "I think we should leave now so that I will not miss my bus home."

When they got up to leave, Kodandaramayya bent and touched Sriramamurthy's feet with reverence, as it is the custom to do bow down to elders when seeking their blessings. Sriramamurthy blessed him again, and both son and father walked out and hurried to Ramachandrudu's house.

As soon as they reached, the meal was served. Sriramulu after saying formal goodbye to Ramachandrudu and his wife thanked them profusely and turned toward his son and said, "Nayana, study well, obey amma and pantulu garu, and serve them well. I will come and visit you soon," Kodandaramayya bent down and touched his father's feet. He saw unspoken emotions in his father's eyes, and his eyes were wet with tears, but he showed extraordinary control over his emotions.

Ramachandrudu said, "Why don't you go to the bus stand and see off your father? I am sure you can find your way back. The other students who are staying here will be coming tomorrow.

They will take you around then." Kodanda nodded his head and immediately went out and put on his chappal without giving Sriramulu a chance to refuse. As father and son walked out, Kodandaramayya took the bag from his father saying, "Nanna, let me carry it."

Preoccupied Sriramulu handed over the cotton bag to his son. They took the rickshaw to the bus stand. Engrossed in their own thoughts, both were silent throughout the rickshaw ride. Suddenly, Sriramulu looked at his son and said, "Nayana, can you go back on your own?"

Kodanda looked a bit annoyed and tried to say with a smile, "Nanna, you are leaving me alone here. How can I manage if I cannot go back on my own? You should stop worrying about me. I am grown up now. It is not like when you left me in Mylavaram." He hoped that he did not come across rudely. Sriramulu also smiled and said mockingly, "Yes, yes, you are grown up, only that I keep forgetting."

Soon, they reached the bus stand. Sriramulu asked, "Should we ask this rickshaw to wait so he can take you back?" Kodandaramayya smiled and said, "Nanna, I will stay with you till the bus leaves. It may be a while, so let him go."

Without further discussion, Sriramulu gave money to the rickshaw puller. When he tried to give some money to his son, Kodanda refused and said, "Nanna, you have already given some at home; I have it in my bag. I don't need more. Please keep it with you or take some chekkarakeli and oranges for amma and sisters. Amma likes sour oranges."

Sriramulu smiled and said, "I will buy fruits for home anyway, keep this extra money in case you need it. Whom will you ask?" and thrust it into Kodandaramayya's hand. Kodandaramayya nodded his head and took the money without fussing. He knew once his father decides, no one could stop him. They walked to the fruit vendor and got some fruits. Sriramulu took two chakkarakeli bananas and put them in his son's hand. Kodandaramayya sensed that his father was restless that he was leaving him behind. But the brave Sriramulu would never show it. The bus Sriramulu had to take arrived soon, and he immediately got into it. He looked at his son and said, "Nayana, now you go, study well, and I will come to see you soon." He turned his head away. Kodandaramayya thought, better I leave now and said, "Nanna, don't worry, I will be good, take care of Amma," and quickly walked away.

He came out of the bus stand, turned back, to look. His father's bus was still there. He felt like going back, but he knew that his father would not be happy with him going back. His father, who always looks and moves forward in life, He felt a wave of affection for his father overtaking him.

He stood there and looked around, some buses coming into the bus stand while others leaving. He saw people waving goodbye to their dear ones, fruit and flower vendors rushing to the buses to sell their wares. Standing there, looking at the new world, Kodandaramayya took it all in. He thought, 'What a big town this is, so much is happening, everyone is preoccupied with their own thoughts.' He slowly walked out of the bus stand toward a rickshaw to go to his new home. Suddenly, a thought came to him as a flash. He thought, 'Why do I need to take a rickshaw? There is so much daylight, I can walk back. I am sure I remember the way back. My father used to walk from Ganapavaram to Mylavaram to see me every day. I am much younger than him; I should not get used to the luxuries and laziness.' He looked at the rickshaw puller who was looking at him enquiringly, smiled and said, "No need now," and walked forward.

He said to himself, 'This is good. I am getting two benefits: saving money while getting good exercise for my body. Two birds with one stone,' and smiled to himself. Since then, Kodandaramayya's marathon walking started, and he walked the maximum distances that he could. He hardly ever took a city bus or evn a rickshaw.

By the time he reached home, it was twilight. As he opened the gate and entered the front courtyard, he saw Ramachandrudu looking anxiously at him. As he climbed the steps leading to the veranda, Ramachandrudu said, "Good, you are home before dark." Kdandaramayya thought that he must have caused him concern. I came walking from the bus stand. "He said I thought I could familiarize the place around."

Ramachandrudu was about to say something, checked himself, and nodded his head with a smile. Later that evening, he said, "It is not a small distance that you walked from the bus stand. Good, walking is the best exercise for your body." Kodandaramayya bent his head and nodded humbly. He thought, 'He was worried and annoyed because I came late, which is understandable.' He has taken up my responsibility and is answerable to my father. At the same time, he is also looking out for my growth. He didn't reprimand me because I would lose my confidence, but he kept quiet to show his displeasure. He let me understand. He didn't praise me at that time because I would not understand that I caused him anxiety. He later praised me to encourage me.

Kodandaramayya went to bed thinking, 'so much has happened in one day.' Though tired, he could not sleep for a while. He missed his parents and chatting away with his mother. He thought about his sisters, thinking how he has to take care of them. 'I have to be strong and work hard to do all I want to achieve.'

The next day, as he woke up at daybreak, he went to the tap outside, brushed his teeth, and took a shower. He washed his clothes, and while drying them on the clothesline, he heard the gate open and saw two boys his age walking in. At the same time, he saw Ramachandrudu coming out onto the veranda from inside the house. He looked at the boys and said, "Oh, you are here. Good, the school will be opening tomorrow. I was wondering when you would come." The boys approached him and joined their hands in greeting. Ramchandrudu now looked at Kodandaramayya as he too approached him and said, "You have already finished your morning chores. That is good."

Turning toward the new boys, he said, "This is Kodandaramayya. He came from Ganapavaram. He will be going to the same school as you both. He joined in the fourth form. After some time, you can take him around." Looking at Kodandaramayya, he introduced the boys, saying, "This is Narasimham. He is in the 5th form, and this is Ramana, who joined in the fourth form like you." Kodandaramayya looked at them, nodded with a smile, and they smiled back. After lunch, Narasimham approached Kodandaramayya and said, "If you want to go around, let's go today. From tomorrow, we will be busy getting ready for school, especially as I will not have much time since I am in the final year and have to work hard."

Kodandaramayya and Ramana both got up and followed him. As they were walking, Ramana asked Kodandaramayya about where he came from and all about his background. Kodandaramayya quickly gave a brief account of his background and asked Ramana where he was from. Ramana said that he was distantly related to Ramachandrudu. He said he was from Ongole, and his father works in the court as a clerk. He added that Narasimham was from Nuzividu, and he belonged to an agricultural family. After going around for a couple of hours, they headed home. The next day, they went and got some books and other essential stationery.

Kodandaramayya woke up earlier than the previous day and got ready by the time others woke up on the first day of school. Ramachandrudu came out and saw that Kodandaramayya was ready. He said, "Good, you are ready. There is time, why don't you go to Kanakadurga temple and come? You know it is not far. By the time breakfast is ready, you can be back. It is your first day of your school."

Kodandaramayya instantly said, "Yes, sir, I will do that and will be back soon." He quickly walked out and headed toward Kanakadurga Devi temple. He walked at a fast pace, and as he reached the temple steps, he literally ran up. Since that day, he would run up the temple stairs and race down every time he went there. During the first year of his stay, he went to the temple almost every day, running up quickly, to have darshan of the deity and run down. Vijayawada became his favourite town. He felt very comfortable and at home in that town.

He came home on time to have his morning meal along with the other boys and Ramachandrudu. All three boys walked to the school together. Kodandaramayya went and met the principal.

New students first meet the principal, who would guide them with some orientation. Kodandaramayya listened to every word the principal said and took it all in. He was then accompanied by a few other students and went to his class.

In the evening, after school, Ramana and Kodandaramayya walked home together. Observing the hustle and bustle of the city, Kodandaramayya thought, "I am far away from home in this big city. I have to avoid temptations and adopt a frugal and active lifestyle."

In Mylavaram, he was an hour's walk away from home. His father would visit him every day for a while, and he would go home every weekend. Now he was here all alone and had to fend for himself completely. He thought, "Any difficulties I face, I have to face them alone. I should not share with my family and burden them. God is with me. I have to be courageous and determined. The biggest gift I got from my parents is discipline."

His day would start at 5 o'clock in the morning. He would wake up, finish his morning chores, and fetch drinking water from the municipal tap a quarter mile from the house. For that, he had to finish his bath in the morning as it was customary. With a wet towel around his waist, he would keep a brass pot filled with water on his head and bring it in the morning before school and in the evening after school. With that water, his teacher's wife would cook food to offer to God daily, before any of them would eat.

Both times, he had to face the sharp sun. In the morning, the rising sun, and the evening sun in the west. He wondered how carrying water was written in his fate, and then reminded himself that in any case, amma (his teacher's wife whom all the students addressed as amma) was cooking food with this water to offer to God. This was his service to God and his teacher. Once a week, his teacher would ask him to buy a coconut for their puja. Sometimes, other students would also bring coconuts, and often theirs would go bad. Ramachandrudu commented, "How come when Kodandaramayya brings the coconuts, they never go bad. These boys are careless and can't choose properly."

Hearing this, Kodandaramayya would smile to himself, thinking, "Amma, what do you know? I constantly pray to God that the coconut should be good and that your puja should not be disturbed. No one knows my trick." He never took any work casually; he always put his heart into whatever he did. Maybe that is the reason he had few regrets in his life but always moved forward and looked to the future.

Two years passed uneventfully. Kodandaramayya was now in SSLC, where he had to appear for the board examinations. Passing SSLC was considered a great achievement. Kodandaramayya could not pass his SSLC exam in the first attempt. He was very sad and felt that he let down his parents. Sriramulu said, "Nayana, show me a handful of people who pass SSLC in the first attempt. It is alright, you will pass next time. You are living away from home, dependent on others' help. I know it is not easy. Now, don't worry about what has happened and look forward. Study harder and you will pass in the next attempt." Yes, Kodandaramayya maintained his resolve, worked hard, and passed his SSLC the following year in 1945. His exemplary and unwavering discipline had helped him in achieving the most difficult tasks of life.

Despite setbacks, Kodandaramayya remained determined and resilient, guided by his principles and the support of his mentors. He faced the future with optimism and a willingness to persevere.

He then joined SRR and CVR college for completing his intermediate course, which was referred to as F.A. (Fellow of Arts) . That course was equivalent of Class 12 and 13 together, during the colonial times.

Whenever he was home, Subbamma would allude to him coming of marriageable age. It was a common practice that both boys and girls got married at quite a young age. Kodandaramayya never took it seriously. He would tease his mother, saying, "Amma, don't you have better things to think about than my marriage!"

Kodandaramayya went home for Dussehra holidays. At home, everyone was excited to see him. His sisters proudly thought, "Our brother is studying in Vijayawada, a big city." They adored their handsome, intelligent, caring, and smart brother.

Kodandaramayya, after waking up in the morning, would wrap a towel around him and pluck the weeds, spread manure in their small vegetable garden, and prune the plants where necessary. His sisters would tag along with him, and he would talk to them about Vijayawada. They would ask, "Annayya, when can you take us to see Vijayawada?" He would smile and say, "Soon, when the time comes."

His mother would get annoyed looking at his clothes and would say, "Why don't you dress properly, wear your pants and shirt? People will come to see you. The villagers are inquisitive about you. They want to know all about your college education and Vijayawada."

Kodandaramayya would answer, "Let them come, I will talk to them and tell them what they want to know. I am not new to them; I grew up in front of their eyes. I am one of them. I don't want them to feel that I have changed and become stylish or that I am showing off."

His mother would get upset, saying, "You have become so independent. You don't listen to me anymore. Do whatever you want." Kodandaramayya would go to his mother, put his hand on her, smile, and say, "I always listen to Amma. Where am I independent? As soon as I get holidays, I run and come to my Amma. I don't go on excursions and picnics with my friends. Come now, smile." Subbamma would hide her smile and say, "Go now, you have become a Chennapatnam takkari." (Chennapatnam, now Chennai, was called Madras during the British rule, and takkari a clever person who fools people with their talk. As Chennapatnam was a big city, people assume that big city folk are clever). This was a favourite phrase of Subbamma. This would happen every time her son came home for holidays.

Chapter 4
FRIENDS FOR LIFE

After the Dussehra holidays, Kodandaramayya returned to Vijayawada. Shortly thereafter he received a letter from his father instructing him to meet his mother's cousins from her maternal side who lived in the city. Initially, Kodandaramayya didn't give it much thought, feeling disconnected from his mother's family. However, a subsequent letter from his father expressed displeasure, mentioning that the relatives had informed him about Kodandaramayya's failure to meet them.

This time, his father provided more details, identifying them as his mother's maternal uncle's sons and emphasizing their closeness to his mother, indicating they could offer valuable support. Sensing his father's annoyance, Kodandaramayya, despite concerns about disrupting his routine, decided to visit them over the weekend. He promptly wrote back to his father, assuring him of his intention to meet the relatives that Sunday and promised to provide an update afterward.

Carefully noting the address, Kodandaramayya found their house. He knocked on their door and was greeted by a fifteen-year-old who looked at him inquisitively. Hesitantly, Kodandaramayya introduced himself as Ganapavaram Sriramulu and Subbamma's son, expressing his desire to meet Dr. Gurunatha Rao and Subbayamma. As he finished his introduction, a woman appeared at the door. As soon as she heard who he was, her face brightened, and she warmly took Kodandaramayya by the hand, exclaiming, "Come, Nayana, you are Subbamma Vadina's son. We have all been eagerly awaiting your visit." Observing the young boy, she introduced him, "He is my younger son, Mohan Rao. My older one, Subba Rao, went out with his uncles. Your mother is my paternal aunt's daughter. We were very close in our childhood, but after our marriages, we couldn't meet much. Go and wash up, it's lunchtime. Gurunatha Rao, my brother, and others will be coming soon. My older brother, Satyanarayana, is also here. He is the one who wrote to your father. Have lunch first, and then we can talk." With those words, she went inside, leaving Kodandaramayya moved by her warmth. He realized that through their relationship, he should address her as Akkayya, elder sister.

As he was talking to Mohan Rao, the front door opened, and two distinguished gentlemen, along with another young boy, entered the house. Kodandaramayya stood up and greeted them. After a brief moment, the older gentleman smiled and exclaimed, "Kodanda!" Kodandaramayya reciprocated with a smile. Both men approached him, putting their arms around him, expressing genuine happiness at his presence. This marked the beginning of Kodandaramayya's enduring relationship with that family. They played a crucial role in supporting him, and were a great source of love and affection throughout his life.

The oldest son of the family, Satyanarayana, faced the challenge of assuming responsibility for the entire family at the young age of 16, following the loss of his father. The family consisted of his mother and three younger brothers. Although they had a reasonable amount of land, its proper management was essential for sustaining the family, which was Satyanarayana's sole responsibility as the other brothers were much younger. At that time, his only sister, a beloved member of the family, became widowed at a very young age bringing a wave of heartbreak to the household. She had two young sons aged three and one, and came to live with them.

Satyanarayana selflessly welcomed his sister and nephews in his care without hesitation, ensuring their well-being. He treated all of his brother's children as his own. Subbayamma, his sister, emanated a divine aura, showering love on everyone she encountered. Her hospitality knew no bounds; she tirelessly cooked and fed anyone who came through their doors, working around the clock to serve all those who crossed her path. Kodandaramayya was related to her from her father's side. He is the son of her first cousin.

Gurunatha Rao, the youngest brother of Satyanarayana, completed his diploma in dentistry and started practicing in Vijayawada. He treated Kodanda like his younger brother. They both took to each other instantly, and they bonded so quickly and deeply that their relationship lasted for life. Subbayamma's sons were younger than Kodandaramayya and looked up to him. Overall, Kodandaramayya was very happy to have found a family so loving and caring. He even visited Alavalapadu, their village, along with Gurunatha Rao. In the second year of the FA, he lived at Subbayamma's house.

Satyanarayana wrote to Sriramulu that finally he met Kodandaramayya and that he was happy to see him, and he found him to be a fine boy. After meeting Kodandaramayya, he immediately thought that Kodandaramayya would make a good match for Satyavathi, his sister-in-law, his wife's sister. The more he thought, he had no doubts about the marriage proposal. He wrote to Sriramulu and his father-in-law, Satyanarayana at Kalavakur, the girl's father.

The girl's family was a bit hesitant initially that Kodandaramayya's family had no property whatsoever. But then Satyanarayana dismissed it, saying that the boy is intelligent, he is getting a good education, the family which is impeccable, is known to them. It is not that they did not have any property; they were also a propertied family, having equal or more land than us, but had only fallen on bad times, and they lost everything. The boy, once he finishes his education, could earn more property than they had. That silenced the girl's uncle and father. With that done, and the girl's family fully satisfied, it was for Sriramulu to go and see the girl and her family.

The girl's family hailed from a village called Kalavakur. Modepally, which is Sriramulu's village, Bodduvane Palem, Subbamma's village, Kalavakur, Alavalapadu, are all within five miles distance from each other, and people considered it as walking distance. Most of the time, they walked the distance between these villages.

Kodandaramayya was unaware of all the marriage discussions, except for his mother telling him whenever he went home for holidays. He would laugh and say, "Amma, what is this talk of marriage? Let me complete my education and start earning." It was common practice that both girls and boys were married at a very young age. They all lived mostly in joint families. It was not important for each individual to earn his living to support the wife or their children. Everything came out of the common pool of money.

When Sriramulu received a second letter from Satyanarayana, he called Subbamma and told her about the situation. She then urged Sriramulu to go and see the girl and her family. Both Sriramulu and Subbamma knew about the girl's family. All of them were distantly related somehow or the other. Subbamma said, "I know the family well. Whenever I visited my sister and my maternal uncle in Alavalapadu, I used to meet this girl's parents often. I used to call her mother amma and her father babu. They are very nice people, please go and see the girl." Sriramulu said, "I will see, when the time comes, it will happen."

Subbamma was annoyed at this and said, "it is always your say, in every matter. Why don't you check the Panchangam and look for a good day? Write a letter to Satyanarayana that you will be coming, so that he can accompany you to go to Kalavakur to see the girl."

Without a word, Sriramulu got up and left. Subbamma looked at her husband, annoyed, and quietly went inside. She knew that his silence indicated serious consideration of the matter and trusted his judgment. Confident in her understanding of her husband, she attended to her chores without further ado.

Two days later, Sriramulu announced that the following day is auspicious and that he was contemplating visiting the girl's family. However, he added that if he encountered any unfavourable signs, he would postpone the visit. Subbamma simply acknowledged his decision, advising him to rest before an early start, if he intended to catch the first bus.

Subbamma and the girls were well aware of Sriramulu's reliance on omens when embarking on new endeavours. They observed as Sriramulu prepared to depart the next day, eagerly awaiting the sign that would affirm his decision. As he opened the gate, they witnessed a beautiful bird flying from left to right in the sky, bringing smiles to their faces. They interpreted this as a positive omen, relieved that things seemed to be aligning favourably. Subbamma bid Sriramulu farewell, urging him to return with good news.

Both the sisters showered their mother with questions. "Father is going to see the girl. If he likes her, he will most probably finalize the match. What about you, amma? Should you not see the girl? You and she are going to be living together. What about Annayya? Is it not important for him to see the girl? What if father says yes, but Annayya does not agree and says he wants to see the girl? Then, what? Father will be upset with Annayya!"

Subbamma heard all their chatter but did not reply. The girls were frustrated and said, "Amma, why are you not talking? This is so important. How come you are not worried?" Subbamma smiled and said, "I know your father. What has to happen will happen! If things go wrong, we will worry then and try to fix it. Why are you unnecessarily making a fuss? Now go and get to your work." She said a bit sternly so that the girls would not continue the conversation. They could do nothing but wait for their father's return.

The mother and daughters waited for Sriramulu's arrival eagerly. Sriramulu returned on the fifth day, spotting their father alighting from the bus. Sita, his younger daughter, fetched a lantern and walked toward him. Sriramulu saw his daughter and said, "I can come without the light, amma. I am used to this path. Why are you bringing the lantern?" and smiled at her affectionately. Sita, without saying much, held her father's hand, and they both walked toward the house.

Sriramulu went to the water tub to wash up. Subbamma handed him a glass of water and said, "Take a breath and take your bath. Hot water is ready, and you can have dinner. I wonder when you ate."

Sriramulu sat down and said, "I am not that hungry. I had some fruits in Vijayawada. I wanted to stop at Vijayawada and see Kodanda, but I thought you would all be worried as it has been 5 days since I left, so I came straight home."

The girls were eagerly looking at their father for the real news. Sriramulu guessed this and smilingly said, looking at Subbamma, "Your son's marriage is fixed. The girl is good looking, the family, we know about them. They are reputed and prosperous family," expressing familiarity and satisfaction with the alliance, he said. In any case the girl's uncle, brother, and Satyanarayana, her father, will be coming to fix the dates and meet us. Mostly, we are thinking the marriage will take place in August."

Saying so, he got up and walked toward the backyard to take a bath. Subbamma said, "How about Kodanda? Should he not see the girl?" she said, walking behind her husband. Sriramulu, immediately said, "Why? If I say so, do you think my son will refuse? I will write to him tomorrow."

Without another word, he walked away. Subbamma and the girls looked at each other. The older daughter, Venkayamma, said, 'See, amma, this is what we were saying.' Without a word, Subbamma walked toward the kitchen to see to dinner arrangements.

Sriramulu once in a while would talk about his journey and give information about the relatives he met. A week later, Sriramulu came into the house while Subbamma was making wicks for lamps and said, "I got a reply from Kodanda. What did I say? He wrote that if I liked the girl, he said that is good enough and that we can go ahead with the preparations as I like. My son is Sriramachandrudu; he will never oppose me." His voice was full of affection for his son, and self-confidence was written all over his face.

Subbamma looked at him and said with a mixture of happiness and sarcasm, "Yes, yes, he is Sriramachandrudu, and you are Dasaradha Maharaja, only there is no kingdom to rule."

Kodandaramayya came home for the holidays. He reached home in the evening. No one talked about the marriage. After dinner, Kodandaramayya sat with his mother to keep her company while she was having dinner. Subbamma said, "Nayana, is it okay if you don't see the girl? Don't be afraid that your father will be upset. We will figure out a way and arrange for you to see the girl."

Kodandaramayya, looking at his mother affectionately, said, "I know your concern. Nanna is happy with the girl and the family.

I trust his judgment. I don't have to see the girl. Now, please relax and let Nanna take care."

Subbamma breathed a sigh of relief. She said the girl's family is coming to meet us soon. Kodandaramayya got up and said, "Amma, you people decide and do what is needed. You have been after me to get married. I agreed, but I am going to continue my studies, and you have to agree to that." Subbamma said, "How is that possible? Once married, we have to bring the girl home. What about her parents? Do you think they all would agree to that?"

Kodandaramayya said, "Amma, first you have to agree, and then we will see about others. Don't take this lightly. I am going to continue my studies. I am going to sleep now; you go to bed soon," and he left. Subbamma did not understand what was going on. She felt too tired to think, and she too went to bed.

The girl's father, uncle, and brother visited Ganapavaram and were highly impressed by Subbamma's hospitality. They had the opportunity to meet Kodandaramayya in Vijayawada on their journey to Ganapavaram, which dispelled any doubts or concerns they may have had. They were very happy to meet Kodandaramayya.

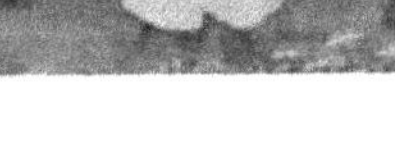

Cousin, Satyanarayana

Gurunatharao, Kodandaramayya, Venkateswarulu

Chapter 5
MARRIAGE AND COMPANIONSHIP

The wedding took place on September 9th, 1947. Time passed swiftly as preparations for the wedding commenced. It is worth knowing about the significant differences between contemporary marriages and those of earlier times. Apart from the traditional rituals and Vedic chants, many formalities have evolved over the years. During those times, hardly anything was readily available. Everything, from grinding various flours to preparing sweets, snacks, pickles, and even procuring ghee, had to be meticulously planned well in advance.

Close family members, especially women such as the bride's or groom's sisters, paternal and maternal aunts, and other relatives with grown up children who did not require constant attention from their mothers, would arrive a month or two before the wedding to assist in preparing all these necessities. Gifts were exchanged only among the immediate family members, and they were typically modest and simple.

Most of relatives were common to both families and lived in close proximity. Lakshamma, Kodandaramayya's aunt's family, came from Chandrala.

The bride, Satyavathi, had many uncles, aunts, and cousins. The wedding of the Karanam's (village karanams are like village heads with the responsibility of maintaining land records and revenue assessments) youngest daughter was celebrated by the whole village, marking the last marriage in the family. All the villagers were invited, along with some government officials. Satyavathi, the youngest child who had never known hardship, was a very intelligent and poised girl, pampered by all.

The day before the wedding, all members of the groom's family arrived. Satyavathi's uncle's house was prepared for the groom and his relatives to stay. That evening, the groom was invited to the bride's house for some rituals. Satyavathi's sister pulled her to the window and showed her Kodandaramayya, the groom, teasingly said, "See him now before it is too late." Satyavathi had a quick glance at her future husband. 'This is it,' she thought. He settled in her heart from that moment, becoming her universe. The world changed for her then.

The next day, during the wedding ceremony, when the veil between the bride and the groom was lifted, Kodandaramayya saw his wife for the first time. As he glanced at her, a smile spread across his face. He thought she was beautiful. "My father did select a beautiful wife for me, thank God," he reflected.

On the night of the wedding, both the bride and groom were taken on a procession in a palanquin all over the village. Kodandaramayya heard people saying, "Our son-in-law is very handsome." He would later tease his wife, saying, "Even your villagers certified that I am good looking. So, you need not have regrets that you didn't see me before the marriage."

Satyavathi would then ask, "What about you? Do you have regrets?" He would reply, "Of course not, I had full faith in my father." Satyavathi would mockingly say, "Thank God for that. If you had seen me, perhaps you would not have agreed."

The next day, the groom's party, along with the bride, her sister, brother, and aunt, went to Ganapavaram as per custom. A few more rituals took place there in the bridegroom's house.

All the villagers in Ganapavaram had been invited for a meal and to bless the groom and bride. The villagers were very happy to see the beautiful bride; she was now the daughter-in-law of their village. Kodandaramayya, along with his wife and her family, stayed in Ganapavaram for 3 days before heading to Kalavakur. After staying there for a couple of days, Kodandaramayya left for Vijayawada to complete the academic year.

Before leaving, he asked, rather told Satyavathi that he wanted to study further and that she would have to either stay with her parents or with his parents. He said, "I will have to go to Visakhapatnam to study B.Com. That will take two years, and then we have to see. I will not be able to take you with me."

She asked, "How often will you be coming to see me?" He smiled and replied, "Whenever I have holidays, I will come and see you." She thought, 'There is no point in me refusing. This is what he wants, let it be. I will not give him any trouble. He wants to do something good, and I need to support him without grumbling.' This had become her habit since then. She never argued or opposed him for anything.

She was a very independent-spirited girl and followed her heart without complaining. In the later years, when one of her children asked her, "Amma, why do you always simply follow father? How come you never oppose him?" to that, she quietly smiled and said, "Why should I oppose him? Yes, sometimes I feel he is not sensitive to my feelings. He does have a short temper, and when things don't get done the way he hopes, he gets unreasonably angry. I do feel hurt. But he is someone who is trying to follow the path of dharma. So, I want to support and follow him, which is good for me too."

She did that all through her life, giving him rock-solid support.

Kodandaramayya worked hard, pursuing his dreams with the determination to achieve what he wanted. He first went to Ganapavaram and told his parents all was well and that his wife had not objected to his studies, and that he would leave for Visakhapatnam to pursue a degree in commerce. Subbamma could not say much but secretly hoped that he would have changed his mind and taken up a job. That, of course, never happened. She hoped that her daughter-in-law would influence her son, as they were newly married, and that he would not leave his wife and go away. With a heavy heart, she bid her son farewell. Kodandaramayya understood his mother's pain but could not find the words to console her.

Subbamma packed all his favourite snacks and pickles as usual before the day of his departure. The whole family gathered in the front yard. His mother said, "Nayana, now you are going far away. I don't know how far Vishakhapatnam is. Take good care of yourself." She could not speak further. Sriramulu noticed and said, "It is enough now. He is not going to have fun and roam around. He is doing this for the betterment of us all. Instead of being brave and encouraging him, why do you do this every time he leaves?" Kodandaramayya quickly moved toward his mother, hugging her and said, "Amma, you know Nanna. Don't mind his words. I understand your pain. Please know that what I am doing will turn out to be the best for all of us. Please bear it for some time, and everything will work out."

His mother nodded her head, and he wiped her tears with her saree. Without any further words, he quickly turned back, walked toward his sisters, put his hand lovingly on their heads, and said, "Study well, and don't bother Amma. Help her as much as you can."

Picking up his bag, he left, while his father walked behind him with the rest of his luggage. He first went to Vijayawada, met Gurunatha Rao and Subbayamma, and took their blessings. Gurunatha Rao said, "Kodanda, I am here for you. Do not hesitate to contact me if you need anything. I will keep in touch with your family. You concentrate on your studies and achieve your goals. We are all very proud of you." He accompanied Kodandaramayya to the railway station.

Kodandaramayya entered another phase of his life in a completely new city. Visakhapatnam is a sea port, very different from Vijayawada. Andhra University is one of the oldest universities in India and the first and foremost in Andhra Pradesh. He stayed in the university hostel and made a few friends but hardly socialized. He would go to the beach often and take long walks to clear his head. He would also visit Ramakrishna Math from time to time.

The Second World War broke out, and India also had to participate, impacting the country significantly. Food was scarce and of poor quality, especially at the hostel. Most of the time, they would serve beaten rice instead of regular rice, twice a day. This caused stomach pain for Kodandaramayya. He did not have much money to eat outside the hostel. Some days, he avoided eating and just drank watery buttermilk so that his stomach would not be bothered by constantly eating the same problematic food.

Time passed by. Sriramulu worked hard on his documentation and taught at the primary school. Kodandaramayya never asked his father for money. Whatever his father sent, he would make do. There were many days when he would miss meals, manage with just two small meals, or sometimes just one meal. No one at home knew about it.

Satyavathi tried to stay most of the time at Ganapavaram, thinking that her husband would write regularly to his parents, and by staying there, she would get his news often.

It was getting more and more difficult for Sriramulu to make ends meet. After the bus service was introduced to Ganapavaram, most of the older students went to Mylavaram for middle and high schools. The fees he would get by teaching higher classes had almost stopped. People were taking produce like fruits, vegetables, even milk, and ghee to the town to sell. Before that, the family was getting plenty of all these things from the villagers, so food was never a problem. Sriramulu found it increasingly challenging to make ends meet.

They would still offer some, but Subbamma understood that they were not as generous as before. She sensed that they were calculating how much money they were losing by giving her a litre of milk. Earlier, they would pour milk into a huge glass without measure and were happy to give. Subbamma decided to buy a buffalo, so she did not want to be dependent on the villagers who were reluctantly sharing. They lost the buffaloes they had when Kanakamma was alive. One died of old age, and the other they had to sell.

She and her husband started growing more vegetables. When they had extra, they would always give it away. One of her neighbours said, "Amma, if you have more vegetables, why don't you sell? I will take them to the market in the town." Subbamma said, "I don't want to sell any vegetables. First of all, we don't have excess, and whatever is left, I want to share with my neighbours who have generously given various things to me when they were not selling."

The one-acre land that they had was providing them with rice for the family. As far as food and other necessities for survival are concerned, they were managing without much difficulty. However, there was no cash flow. Subbamma was also worried about the girls, their education, and their marriages. These thoughts never crossed Sriramulu's mind. Even if they occurred sometimes, he would push them away, thinking that his son would take care of all that. His first priority was to help him complete his education. Sriramulu's second daughter was very keen on studies. Whenever she could, she would sit with her books while the older daughter was more interested in learning songs, listening to her mother's stories from Ramayana and Mahabharatha. She was always learning to draw difficult muggulu and was happy when she could master some difficult ones.

Sriramulu had to borrow money often to send to his son. Whenever he earned a reasonable amount for his document writing, he would return the money to the debtors. People who loaned him respected him and had faith in him. They also thought that the money was being spent for a good cause, and once Kodandaramayya finished his education, he would be able to take care. So, they didn't hesitate to give loans to Sriramulu. Moreover, Sriramulu had a reputation of being a hardworking, honest, and a wise person.

All the collective hard work of Kodandaramayya, his parents, and the endurance of Satyavathi, in staying away from her husband for so long, right after the marriage paid off and he successfully completed his B.Com.

He tried hard to find employment after completing his degree. Things did not work as he thought. He did not get any job offer but had unpleasant experiences in his job search, which made him decide to pursue a digree in Law, which would open more doors to employment as well as enable him to practice law independently.

Kodandaramayya with his wife Satyavathi

Satyavathi's brother, Narasimha Rao with his wife,
Sakunthala

Chapter 6
ON THE PATH TO BECOMING A LAWYER

Kodandaramayya didn't realize when he drifted into slumber, amidst his childhood reminiscences. He reached Madras, two days before the college reopened. He headed directly to the accommodations he had arranged while he was in Madras, along with two other fellow students who were also starting their legal studies. He went walking to the college from his place to see if it was possible to walk to the college every day. After reaching, he realized that it was quite a distance from his room, especially if he had to attend morning classes; it would be very difficult to reach on time. He thought he had no choice but to take a tram or a bus. There was no way that he could avoid the transport expenses. Then he thought, "I will try to find another house soon close to the college. But for now, I have to manage." Kodandaramayya felt that, "Somehow, I am developing a nature not to worry or think too much about the situations when it cannot be helped or avoided. Maybe it's from my father, I learned this subconsciously." Sriramulu always looked into the future and took necessary steps without thinking too much about the past.

Kodandaramayya spent most of his free time visiting the beach and would go to Kapaleswara temple whenever he could. He also would frequently go to the Theosophical Society and borrowed books from there to read. He made a few acquaintances, especially with Telugu-speaking people who were residing in Madras. Two years passed quickly and uneventfully. He visited Ganapavaram four or five times during his holidays in those two years. During that time, Satyavathi stayed in Ganapavaram because Kodandaramayya was visiting Ganapavaram more often.

Kodandaramayya completed his two years of law and arrived at the last term. The last term fees and the exam fees had to be paid before appearing for the exams. Kodandaramayya tried his best to raise at least some money without troubling his father. He tried hard, but those were the times when not many people had excess money. All the people he knew were students studying along with him and a couple of others who were doing their jobs. No one could help him. He had no other choice but to go home and talk to his parents.

He reached Ganapavaram on a Saturday evening. His parents and sisters were surprised to see him and wondered what must have happened that suddenly he arrived without a sending them a letter in advance. Satyavathi was in Kalavakur at that time. Subbamma looked at her son's face and said, "Nayana, how are you? Is everything okay? You look very tired. Wash up; we can talk later.

As they were talking, Sriramulu walked through the gate with a bag of fresh vegetables in his hand. Kodandaramayya thought, "Oh, Nanna is coming from the farm, bringing fresh vegetables." He quickly reached his father and took the bag from his hand. Sriramulu saw his son and was pleasantly surprised. He asked with a little nervousness, "Nayana, how come you are here? Do you have any holidays? I thought your exams would be starting soon. What is this? You did not even write a letter?"

Kodanda said, "Everything is alright, Nanna. I don't have any holidays now. You are right, my exams are approaching soon. I need to talk to you and Amma. We will sit and talk after dinner.

You must be tired after the day's work. Let us both have our bath and have dinner." Turning to Subbamma, he said, "Amma, what are you making for dinner? I will have to leave tomorrow or the day after, as soon as I can. So, you have to make everything you want to feed me in these two days."

Smiling, he went into the backyard to check on the plants. He always did that whenever he came home. Sriramulu and Subbamma looked at each other, but without a word, they left to attend to their work.

Kodandaramayya spent some time with his sisters, checking on their studies. As usual, the younger sister had many questions and lots of inquiries about the university and Madras. She wanted to know the university environment, the difference between the college in Vijayawada and the university in Madras. She asked her brother if she could also go and study there when she grows up. Kodandaramayya smiled and said, "There's a lot of time to go there. Yes, study well, and when the time comes, you can certainly do that," he patted her on the back and looked at his older sister, smiled and said, "Now what about you? Still the same not interested in studies. You need to have a minimum degree, Amma. Try and do it." His sister smiled shyly and nodded her head.

At dinner, Sriramulu and Kodandaramayya, and the girls sat down to eat. Subbamma, sitting with all the dishes spread in front of her, served her husband and children. They all ate, everyone engrossed in their own thoughts. Sriramulu finished his dinner first and went and sat down in the front veranda. After Subbamma finished her dinner, the girls started cleaning up the kitchen. Kodandaramayya went and sat with his father, and his mother soon joined them.

Kodandaramayya noticed that his mother joined them very quickly and asked her, with concern in his voice, "Amma, you are here already. Did you eat properly?" Subbamma said, "I had a very late lunch, Nayana. I'm not very hungry. Now, tell us what is on your mind." Subbamma pulled a stool and sat down. Sriramulu, said, "Your brother-in-law wrote that Satyavathi wants to come here. You know that she went for the Sankranti festival. It has been three months." Kodandaramayya said, "It is okay, Amma. Just some more time and everything will be settled soon. We all have to go through these difficult times. She will be okay. You don't worry." Subbamma said, "Poor girl, running between the two places. Now, tell us what is on your mind."

Kodandaramayya looked at her parents and said, "Nanna, a few more days and I will be completing the course and getting my Law degree. I have worked hard and will surely pass. Then I have a one-year apprenticeship, during which time I will also be paid some money. Now I have to pay the exam fees and the last term fees, which are due. I will not be able to sit for the exam if I don't pay the complete fees. I tried my best to tell them that I could pay some amount now and then some later. They did not agree as this is the final year. They feel that once a student completes the exams, he will not go back, and they will not be able to collect the fees, which is understandable. They have been very helpful so far towards me. Whenever I paid the fees, they did not collect any late fees. They gave me a week of extra time until the day before the exams. I tried to borrow from people I know. I could not get any help from them as they had their own problems. I understand this is a difficult situation."

After a few minutes, Subbamma said, "How can we get that much money in such a short time?" Sriramulu, immediately said, "We don't have to discuss anything now." Looking at Kodandaramayya, he said, "Nayana, we will do what is needed. I am going to bed now, so should you both." He got up and left with finality in his voice. Kodandaramayya, and his mother, knew that it was a command and nothing further would happen. No one would speak after that. They both looked at each other in silent anticipation and quietly went to bed.

Kodandaramayya looked at his father, who was lying down on the next cot, and felt an unknown sadness. He thought, 'My father is getting old, still struggling to make ends meet, but his courage is boundless. He did not show a glimpse of anxiety after I told him about the college situation. I will soon have to take the burden off him,' and then he slept without further thoughts.

When he woke up in the middle of the night, he saw his father sitting on the bed. He got up immediately and asked, "Nanna, why are you not sleeping? Are you okay?" Sriramulu said, "Oh, I am all good. I got up to go to the bathroom." He lay down on the bed without a word and turned to the other side without giving room for any conversation. Kodandaramayya also could not sleep, thinking about their financial situation. He wondered if he took the right decision to go for further studies. It took a while for him to fall asleep.

By the time he woke up, it was later than usual. He noticed that everyone was up and busy with their morning chores. He did not see his father around. He went to his mother, who was milking the cow. This task is normally done by Sriramulu. Kodandaramayya looked at his mother and said, "Amma, where is Nanna? Where did he go so early without even milking the cow?" Subbamma smiled and said, "You know your father, if something gets into his mind, he never wastes any time. He said that he had some work and he had to go, and asked me to take care of this. Anyway, now you go and brush. Meanwhile, I will get the milk ready for you all," and she went inside.

Without going into the house, Kodandaramayya started cleaning the cow shed quietly. He asked his sister, who was plucking flowers for Subbamma's pooja, to bring him a towel. After cleaning, he had a quick bath. As he was entering the house,

Subbamma said, "What is this? You are here for a day, why do you have to do all this? You did not even have a glass of milk." Kodandaramayya smiled and said, "Why, Amma? Can I not do this work? I had my bath; I can have my milk now." As they were talking, Sriramulu entered the house. He said, "Both of you, mother and son, come here, I have something to tell you."

They sensed urgency in his voice and walked toward him. If it were another time, Subbamma would have said, "You are always in a hurry. I have so much work to do. Hold on, we will be there in a bit." But this time, it was different. Without a word, both of them walked toward Sriramulu, who sat on the stool in the front veranda.

Sriramulu asked them to sit down, and both the mother and son sat down on the mat, which was in front of Sriramulu. Without much introduction, Sriramulu said, "I have arranged the money, Nayana. You may have to wait for one more day. The buyer needs 2 days' time to get the money." Both Subbamma and Kodandaramayya said at the same time, "What buyer?"

Sriramulu said, "What do you mean," what buyer? I sold the land, our farm. I thought about it a lot. Where can I get that amount now? After paying the fees, we can survive for six months or one year with the remaining money. After that, God will help and show us some way. By then, Nayana will also complete his education and start work."

Looking at Subbamma, he said, "Why do you look so shocked?" This is not the time to waver. Once Nayana finishes his education and gets his law degree, all will be fine. Let us not go back and forth now. The decision is made, nothing more to think about." Turning toward Kodandaramayya, he said, "Nayana, we need a day or two to arrange the money. I asked them to give whatever is required for you to take with you now. The rest, they will give us whenever we require."

Subbamma could not contain herself. She said, "Without even telling us a word, how come you took this decision? Just on that one acre we have been surviving. Even if we did not have anything, we could get some rice and vegetables. It has been sustaining us. What about the girls? Did you think about their future? Is that not important?" She could not talk further. Sriramulu got very angry. He said, "What would you have done if I told you? You could have said the same thing. Do you have any other solution? Do you understand the situation? This is the way you always talk, and then everyone gets hurt. Go and start your cooking, I will have to go out again."

Thus saying, he quickly walked away from there. Subbamma, with tears in her eyes, quickly went inside the house. Kodandaramayya, watching everything, could not say a word. He quickly gathered himself and walked behind his mother. He stood in front of her and said, "Amma, you know Nanna's anger. Is this anything new? I completely understand your anxiety. At this point, it looks like we have no other choice. Amma let me finish my course. You have to have faith in me. Please don't worry, we will get through this. I will take care of my sisters. I know it is very painful to let go of the little property that we have. I also understand that you are upset as I have not taken up the job after my graduation. Believe me, being a professional will have its own advantages. Please don't worry now and have faith. We will get through this."

Subbamma looked at her son and said, "Nayana, don't mistake me. In my anxiety, I said something irrelevant. Of course, you are there, and you will take care of everything. My worry is also that how much burden we can place on your shoulders. Anyway, I need nothing more than to see you succeed, and God willing, we will all be okay. Now let me go and do my cooking quickly; otherwise, your father will come and dance," she added smilingly, "Don't worry. Will you be going and seeing Satyavathi before you go to Madras?"

Kodandaramayya said, "No, Amma, not now. I will go directly to Madras, finish my exams, and come. By then, she can come here, or I will go and bring her. We can all stay for some time before I start my apprenticeship."

Then he walked into the backyard where his father was giving the calf its feed of grass. Kodandaramayya took it from his hand and said, "Nanna, give it here, let me do it. You go have your bath and pooja." Hesitantly, he said, "Nanna, are you sure about what you are doing?" Sriramulu smiled and said, "Of course, I thought about it thoroughly. I know what I am doing. Now you stop thinking about it and concentrate on your studies. Don't worry about what your mother said; she is just anxious."

Kodandaramayya said, "It is okay, Nanna, don't be so hard on her. I know you both want what is good for me and for the family. I will finish my studies, and hopefully, I will be able to take care of everything," Sriramulu said, "Enough talk now, go and see your mother. If she has finished cooking, I will take a bath and get ready for my pooja." Then he turned and walked away. Kodandaramayya knew that that was the end of the conversation.

By late evening, Sriramulu brought the cash and gave it to Kodandaramayya and said, "If you want to leave now, the last bus is at 10 o'clock. You can still take that bus and go." Kodandaramayya said, "No, Nanna, that's not necessary. I will take the early morning bus, reach Vijayawada, and then take the 4 o'clock afternoon train to Madras from Vijayawada. No point leaving now."

Subbamma came and said, "Good Nanna, I'll have some time to get you some snacks ready for you. I don't want you to rush like this. You will have something to eat when you are studying for your exams. Come sit with me while I prepare them." Sriramulu looked at her and said, "Yeah, you and your snacks, that will never stop," and left.

Kodandaramayya, as he was leaving the next day, went to his sisters and said, "As soon as I finish my studies, I will set up practice. I will take you both and join you in the school. Help Amma and look after Nanna. They both are aging. I will ask your sister-in-law to come here." And then looking at Subbamma, he said, "Amma, all will be okay," and touched her feet, seeking her blessings. Then he turned to his father and took his blessings too.

Kodandaramayya came back to Ganapavaram after successfully completing the course. Satyavathi was also there at Ganapavaram. The whole family had a nice time together. He stayed at Ganapavaram until his results came. Many people from the village came and talked to him, took his advice about the studies of their children; many of them wanted to know about Madras. They called it Chennapattanam in those days. Subbamma cooked to her heart's content for the children. The girls were very happy to have their brother and sister-in-law with them.

Results were announced, and Kodandaramayya passed his law exams. All the hardships the family went through have finally given the expected positive results. All were happy in their own way. Everyone in the family and the villagers too were ecstatic. He was the first person who became a professional, a lawyer in their village. Eventually, the holidays came to an end, and the time came for Kodandaramayya to leave for his apprenticeship.

Sriramulu told his son, "Take Satyam and leave her with her parents. It has been a while since she came. Now that you are also leaving, it is appropriate for you to meet your in-laws and take their blessing."

Kodandaramayya was a bit reluctant to go. He somehow sensed that his father-in-law was not too happy about him going for further studies without taking up a job. That was a bit unpleasant to him. He said nothing to his father. Sriramulu sensed that Kodandaramayya was not keen on going to Kalavakur. He called Kodanda in private and said, "I am feeling that you are reluctant to go to Kalavakur. It is not right. They are your wife's parents; you have to give them utmost respect, no matter what. I want you to always remember this."

When Kodandaramayya heard this, his respect for his father grew further. He thought, "What a righteous man my father is, always trying to do the right thing." Interestingly, he remembered his mother teasing him and his father, saying that he is Sri Ramachandrudu, and his father Dasaratha maharaja, and that none of them have any kingdom. He smiled to himself and thought, 'Yes, I do adore my father.' He then immediately said, "Sure, Nanna, I will do as you say, take Satyam with me, leave her there, and go to Madras."

That settled, Sriramulu looked at the Panchangam and said the time for your departure is good in two days. The day they were leaving, as usual, Subbamma filled the bags with snacks for Kodandaramayya and also for Satyavathi's family. Kodanda and Sriramulu, along with the rest of the family, even the neighbours, wondered how she managed to do so much with the little money she had. She never sent any neighbour away empty-handed when they came for something, be it for a pickle, a snack, or even some grains.

Two days later, Kodandaramayya and Satyavathi headed for Kalavakuru, Satyavathi's parents' village. The girls were sad to see their sister-in-law leaving. Satyavathi went to them and said, "Don't feel bad, as soon as your brother finishes his apprenticeship, we will all stay together." Looking at her younger sister-in-law, she said, "You can join a good school. I know you are looking forward to going to a proper school. Now take care of Amma and Nanna."

Satyavathi quickly turned back, went to her mother-in-law and father-in-law, and took their blessings by touching their feet. She walked toward the wooden gate following her husband with mixed feelings. Happy to see her loving family, but at the same time, sad to leave this family she belonged to now. Again, her husband would be away; she did not know for how long.

Sriramulu followed them to the bus stop. Once they got onto the bus, he waved at them smiling. Kodandaramayya looked at his father. He thought, 'Nanna is looking tired. God, help me to quickly take the burden off his shoulders.' He too quietly waved at him as the bus was leaving.

As they reached Vijayawada, it was about 10 o'clock. They went straightaway to Subbayyamma's house. Subbayyamma and Satyavathi are first cousins. They stayed there that night and headed to Kalavakur the next day early morning. They had to change two more buses from Vijayawada to reach the village. Sriramulu wrote a letter informing Satyavathi's family about their arrival. Narasimha Rao, Satyavathi's elder brother, was waiting for them with the bullock cart at the bus station in Addanki town to take them to their village, which was five miles away.

Satyavathi was thrilled to see her brother, who was her favourite. It was her brother who homeschooled her. Even in those days, he taught her how to read and write Hindi, encouraged her to read Telugu literary classics, and told her about the political situation at the time. Through him, Satyavathi learned a lot about the independence movement. He insisted that everyone should wear Khadi clothes. She was very close to both her brother and her sister-in-law. All three of them reached home by lunchtime.

Everyone was happy to see their daughter and son-in-law. Satyavathi's mother and sister-in-law got busy with preparing special food. Kodandaramayya spent two nights there and planned to leave the next day. That night, Satyavathi said, "So this is it. When will I see you again? I am asking so I can prepare mentally, not to bother you."

Kodandaramayya looked at his wife, and his heart melted. He thought, 'She never complains, always accommodating, and only thinks of helping me and encouraging me.' He then said, "How about I stay back for a couple of days more and go directly to Madras instead of staying in Vijayawada? Satyavathi said Gurunatha Rao bava may be disappointed; you both are very close; he may miss you."" Kodandaramayya smiled at his wife and said, "Don't worry about that. I will explain to him; he will understand." Satyavathi's heart beat fast. That was the first time she felt that her husband openly wanted to do something for her. Kodandaramayya used to tease her that he married her without even meeting her or seeing her. Satyavathi, after hearing her husband say this several times, she said, "Yes, that is true, but I too have married you without seeing you." Even in those days, the boy and girl would, at times get a chance to speak to each other before the marriage. Many a time, the matches were fixed with families known to each other so at some point or the other; they would meet in family gatherings. This was not the case with the both of them, they were strangers to each other when they were married, and yet a steady affection grew.

Kodandaramayya somehow did not expect this. He just thought, "I am such an obedient son; I married as per my father's wishes, unlike the boys of these times," and felt good about it. He was taken aback, and suddenly it hit him that he had been thinking from his side alone. He was also thrilled at his wife's reply: 'smart and, at the same time, without being rude, she expressed her feelings assertively.' He further thought, 'Not once did she oppose me in any matter. She never complained that she had to stay away from me endlessly. She either stayed at her in-laws or at her parent's place, which is not a pleasant thing for a married girl.'

He further thought patiently and quietly, 'She has been supporting me. I could do all these things because of her unconditional devotion for me.' Two days went by very fast. Satyavathi's family also felt very happy that Kodandaramayya could spend some time with them and that they got to know him better.

Satyavathi was a bit under the weather for the next two days. Everyone thought that she must be missing her husband, and they all felt that she had been very patient and brave. They also felt that Kodandaramayya was prolonging his professional training too much and were a bit annoyed.

Two days later, when the village doctor, who was also a family friend, came to visit them, Satyavathi's father said to him, "Kotayya, go and see Sathyam. She has been feeling a bit low ever since she came from her in-laws' house." Kotayya went inside and saw Satyavathi sitting with her sister-in-law and asked Satyam, "How are you? Let me check your pulse."

Satyavathi said, "I am alright and may be a little bit tired because of my travel," and extended her hand. Kotayya checked her pulse, looked at her, smiled, and called to her sister-in-law, saying, "Sakunthalamma, come over here." Sakunthalamma was a bit agitated, wondering what the matter could be. As soon as they entered the front room, Kotayya looked at her, smiled, and said, "Your sister-in-law is joining the forces; she is pregnant." Sakunthalamma, with a sigh of relief, said, "That is very good news; let me tell others,"And walked out in a hurry. She too was pregnant at that time. The whole family was happy to hear the news.

Satyanarayana, Satyavathi's father wrote to Sriramulu first, as it is customary to inform the elders of the family. He then wrote to Kodandaramayya about the good news. On hearing the news, everyone in Ganapavaram was thrilled. The girls were happy that they were going to have a little baby at home.

Sriramulu also wrote to Kodandaramayya. Kodandaramayya thought, "How come I am getting a letter as I just returned from home? Father must have some important news." He wondered and hoped that all is well at home. He opened the letter. As soon as he read the letter, he thought of his wife and wished that he was with her at this time. 'So, I am going to be a father.' The next day or so, he received a letter from his father-in-law as well. He immediately wrote to his father and his father-in-law, saying that he was happy to hear the news and hoped that Satyavathi is healthy. He then said he will visit them as soon as he can.

He then fell into his work with full gusto. Eswara Venkatesam, who was a lecturer at Visakhapatnam from Andhra University, moved to Madras to practice law in the High Court. Kodandaramayya knew him from his college days when he was doing B.Com. Kodandaramayya had met him several times. When the time came for his apprenticeship, he approached Mr. Venkatesam. He welcomed Kodandaramayya and took him into his office. During that time, people normally never got paid. Knowing Kodandaramayya's situation, Mr. Venkatesam paid him 50 rupees per month. He also introduced one Mr. Vishnu Rao, another senior advocate who lived in the next street. Kodandaramayya would go there every day in the evening and would work there too. He would get paid a hundred rupees from there. Altogether, he would get a hundred and fifty rupees per month. Somehow, his rent, food, and transport expenses were covered. He would save twenty to thirty rupees per month.

After six months of apprenticeship, he took a week off and went home. He wanted to meet his family as well as his pregnant wife. He first went to Ganapavaram. He stayed there for three days and got pampered by his parents and his sisters, who were glad to see him.

This time, he went and visited his aunt in Chandrala. His aunt, as usual, mocked her sons, saying, "See my nephew; he'll be an advocate soon." As usual, Kodandaramayya came to the defence of his cousins, saying, "If they are not here to take care of all the property, what would happen? As I don't have any property, what would I do but study?" His aunt laughed and said, "Enough of you supporting them. Let me get you something to eat,"

He spent a couple of hours with them. Walking back, he was happy he made this visit. After three days, he left Ganapavaram for Kalavakuru to see his wife. Subbamma did not say anything this time. She just gave her blessings and as he left. He thought, 'How come amma did not say anything about my studies and bringing her daughter-in-law?' Then he thought she must have been tired, and he felt a little sad and helpless.

Kodandaramayya found himself pressed for time, so he was unable to inform his in-laws in advance of his arrival through a letter. Any correspondence would have inevitably reached them after he had already arrived.

He took a bus to Vijayawada and from there had to take another bus to Addanki. Then, he either had to walk or engage a bullock cart to reach Kalavakur. As he did not inform anyone earlier, he thought, 'There will not be any transport for me, so I have to walk.' He hoped that he would be able to reach before nightfall. When he alighted from the bus at Addanki, he saw the sun set and there was a light drizzle. Kodandaramayya did not know what to do. He could meet someone in Addanki and ask for help. Almost everyone knew his father-in-law in Addanki. For some reason, Kodandaramayya decided not to ask anyone, and planned to walk quickly and reach Kalavakur in an hour.

He thought, 'Why bother anyone? It is a straight road. I have been on this road a few times. I will walk quickly,' he decided, as walking was never an issue with him. As Kodandaramayya started walking, the rain began to pour in heavy showers and darkness enveloped him. 'I hope I did not take a wrong decision in haste', he thought. At one point, he could not move further. He located a tree when there was a flash of lightning, and managed to stand under it. At the next flash of lightning, he felt a log or some kind of rock, with his hand and sat on it. Thunder and lightning continued unabated.

The rain slowed down, but it was still pitch dark. When the next flash of lightning came, he saw that he was, after all, on the road. He thought, "I should slowly start walking as the rain seems to be receding." As he extended his hand to get his bag, in another bright flash of lightening he realized to his horror, that his bag was right by a snake hill. He quickly grabbed it, got up, and started walking in a daze. After taking a few steps, he calmed down and was grateful that he was protected by God. He thought, 'My parents' blessing, my wife's goodness, and my unborn child's luck protected me.' He stopped for a bit and again started walking. He saw some flickering lights of a village at a distance and thought, 'Finally, I am getting close to some habitat; that is good. Even if it is not Kalavakur, it is some village.'

As he continued walking, suddenly he saw someone with a light approach him from behind. He stopped as torchlight was focused on him, and he tried to figure out who that person was. Kodandaramayya looked at the villager and asked if it was the village Kalavakur. He wanted to make sure, as he was worried that he might have walked to the wrong village.

Looking at Kodandaramayya, the man thought, 'Who is this stranger coming to our village in this tempest?' He looked hard at Kodandaramayya, focusing the light on his face, and rudely said, "Yes, this is Kalavakur, but who are you? Coming to our village at this hour and in such weather, what was so urgent that you walked through the forest at such a time?"

Kodandaramayya was a little irritated with these questions and by the rudeness in his voice. He was exhausted, cold, and tired. He did not feel like answering the stranger's questions. Without a word, he turned and kept walking. The villager came closer and said, "Hey, you! Why are you not answering?"

Kodandaramayya as he continued walking, muttered back "It does not matter who I am, all I wanted to know is whether this was Kalavakuru or not." The villager was very annoyed. He thought with some irritation, 'Who is this guy? He has no manners. Maybe I should just whack him. Being a stranger coming to my village, how dare he speak to me like this?' The man too was tired and cold. Drenched in the storm after a hard day's work, when he was about to go home, he got stuck in the rain. He quietly followed Kodandaramayya, who noticed that he was being trailed. He wanted to turn back and say something but was too tired to speak.

He quickly walked toward his father-in-law's house, thinking, "Whoever this person is and whatever his intention is, the light from his torchlight, is helping me walk in the dark." He suddenly felt bad. He thought, 'I should not have been rude to him. After all, it is normal for anyone to be curious when you come across a stranger in your village.' He once turned back to smile at the villager, but it was too dark to see his face. He quickly walked and reached home.

As Kodandaramayya entered the house without hesitation, the man behind was curious and athe same time anxious. 'Who is he? He must be known to Karanam garu from the way he is entering the house without hesitation. Oh my God, what was I thinking? Maybe he is someone important.'

Narasimha Rao, Kodandaramayya's brother-in-law noticed someone entering the house. He was coming into the main hall after finishing dinner. He called out, "Who is there?" He could not see in the darkness. There were no electric lights to light the whole room in those days. Kodandaramayya responded swiftly, "It is me, Kodandaramayya."

Narasimha Rao quickly came to the door with a lantern in his hand and showered Kodandaramayya with questions filled with concern. "Come in, come in. You are drenched. Are you alright?

How come you did not send us a message? How did you come in this heavy rain and at this hour?" He was clearly worried. He called out to the family, saying, "Come out, Kodandaramayya is here. Bring a towel, he is all drenched."

Satyavathi, his mother, and wife rushed out. Kodandaramayya had said, "Oh, I am alright, don't worry, I just got wet in the rain." Taking the towel from Sakuntala, Narasimha Rao's wife, he said, "As it has been almost six months since I came home, I decided to visit my parents and also come here. I did not have time to write a letter as I made a sudden decision."

He then turned to the villager who was standing quietly, shivering, and said, "This man here has been very helpful in bringing me home." The man stood there, looking aghast. Narsimha Rao walked up to the man and, looking at him, said, "Oh, it is you, Narayana. What is going on? Where did you meet my brother-in-law?"

Narayana folded his hands and said, "Today has been a lucky day for me. I got stuck in the rain on my farm. I was waiting for the rain to stop when I saw someone coming in the rain toward our village whom I had never met before. I thought he was a stranger. I wondered, 'Who is this person coming to our village at this time?' When I asked him who he was, I did not get a proper reply. I got angry and thought of whacking him, but I controlled myself and decided to follow him to see what was going to happen. 'God was kind to us,' he said, with tears in his eyes.

He then turned to Kodandaramayya and said, "I am really sorry. I could not recognize you." Kodandaramayya came close to him, smiled, and said, "So your name is Narayana? It is ok, Narayana. I was also very tired, and I was rude too. I should have answered you properly. It is, after all, your village, and I am a stranger. Now, don't worry. Go home quickly; you too are drenched and cold." Narasimha Rao, looking at Narayana, said,

"No harm done, now all are safe. It is good that you accompanied my brother-in-law with the light."

He walked into the kitchen, to check how far the dinner preparations had come for the son-in-law of the house. After taking a bath with hot water, Kodandaramayya narrated the whole adventure while having his dinner. He was happy to see everyone, especially his wife who was six months pregnant at that time. He said, "By the time the baby comes and you are ready to join me, I will finish my apprenticeship. I will rent a proper house, and you can then come. Now I live in a small single room. There is talk that the court will be moving to Guntur. Actually, it will be convenient for all of us if that happens."

Satyavathi did not talk much, she just listened. Somehow, the pregnancy made her very quiet. She was a bit worried and confused. She was immersed in her thoughts and the daunting future, 'For all of this to work out, it would be a year or two before she could move in with her husband'.

It occurred to her that she had to get through this pregnancy and then, after delivering her child, would need to remain with her parents for at least six months. She thought, 'Well, let everything happen the way it should. I should not think beyond that which I can not control.' When Kodandaramayya looked at Satyavathi, he felt pained at leaving his pregnant wife behind.

Kodandaramayya bid farewell to all of them after two days and left for Madras. After reaching Madras, he got completely immersed in his work. Mr. Venkatesam, was very happy with the hard work, sincerity, and dedication with which Kodandaramayya worked. Kodandaramayya successfully completed his apprenticeship in 1951.

In the year 1952, he was enrolled at the bar as an advocate. And joined Mr. Venkatesam as his first junior. He informed his family at Ganapavaram and Kalavakur, and all were ecstatic.

Later, one of Kodandaramayya's colleagues, Mr. Adinarayana Raju, said, "Intelligent people are usually not this hard-working; they get bored easily and are easily satisfied with whatever they do. Kodandaramayya, on the otherhand was intelligent as well as hard-working." He further said, "With both these essential qualities, Kodandaramayya could achieve what he has achieved. Given his circumstances and the challenges he faced, he performed a herculean task". Perhaps that is the reason why Mr. Venkatesam let Kodandaramayya work in another office as well, to build his experience and earn extra money to support his family.

During the period of his apprenticeship, he developed a profound interest and started reading law journals as well as law textbooks in depth.

Kodandaramayya worked hard and pursued his discipline with great zeal and enthusiasm. His only breaks from his work were to go to the beach sometimes, visit the Kapaleshwara temple, and attend talks in philosophical group once in a while. He developed a reading habit around this time. He would primarily read biographies of eminent people and started reading spiritual books, which he would borrow from the library at the Theosophical Society.

Chapter 7
FATHER

One night, he had a dream that he was in the attic of his home in Ganapavaram. He saw an elderly lady with a big Bottu (a red mark women wear on their forehead) on her forehead holding a basket in her hand. When she saw him, she smiled. Looking at her, he felt that she was the Goddess Parvati. He exclaimed loudly, saying, "Devi, you have come!" and jumped down from the attic, and began praying to her. He suddenly woke up from his dream. The next day, he received the news that he was blessed with a daughter. He believed that his dream indicated he was going to have a daughter. He immediately decided to name his daughter Parvathi. He thought gratefully, 'I have become a professional and a father at the same time. I have been blessed. This is a very important time in my life.'

It took him almost six months to go and see the child. Sriramulu sent him letters insisting that he visit Kalavakur soon. He wrote to him, "Go and see your child, perform the naming ceremony, and bring my granddaughter and daughter-in-law home."

Kodandaramayya also received a letter from his father-in-law and brother-in-law. They too felt that he needed to set everything aside now and go see the child and do what was necessary. 'It has been almost a year since he saw Satyam. He realized that no matter how patient and understanding she is, he should not delay being with her any further. I want to see my daughter and my wife,' he thought. He then wrote to his father-in-law, suggesting that they could decide on the date for the naming ceremony and inform him so that he could be there.

All were happy to hear that he was coming. The date was decided by the priest. Sriramulu also came from Ganapavaram. Kodandaramayya arrived two days prior ro the ceremonies. After the function, Satyavathi's mother and brother accompanied her to Ganapavaram, as it is the tradition that the girl is not sent to her in-laws home alone after the delivery. At Ganapavaram, both the girls and Subbamma were eagerly awaiting the arrival of the little girl.

The girls were so ecstatic to see their niece. They decorated the cradle with leaves and flowers. The youngest daughter of Sriramulu, Sita, couldn't wait to see her niece. Kodandaramayya noticed that Satyavathi was looking a bit low. He thought that taking care of the baby and delivery must have taken a toll on her. He asked her what was wrong. Satyavathi, as usual, responded that she was fine.

Kodandaramayya said, "I am assisting my seniors at the court. Once I start taking up cases independently, I will be able to sustain myself financially. I will take you to Madras soon. Just wait a couple of months more. There is also talk that the High Court may move to Andhra Pradesh, to Guntur; if that happens, it will be easy for all of us. We will immediately rent a house there and we can set up the family." Satyavathi, as usual, nodded her head in agreement.

Three days later, Kodandaramayya left for Madras. A few months passed, and everyone fell into their routine. Satyavathi remained in Ganapavaram. She did not go to her mother's place for more than six months.

Kodandaramayya worked hard. He would spend hours studying cases, and he also took delight in reading other literature.

He tried to send home some amount of money every month. In the middle of all this, there was talk of moving the High Court to Andhra Pradesh, which made Kodandaramayya rethink his decision of taking Satyavathi to Madras. He wondered if it would be better to wait. Somehow a year and a half passed by quickly. Kodandaramayya tried to visit Satyavathi more frequently than he did before, but could not due to work pressure.

One day, he got a telegram from Vijayawada saying that Satyam was unwell and he must visit her immediately. Kodandaramayya, worried and uncertain, informed Mr. Venkatesam and caught the next train. He thought, "Something was bothering her. She was not herself when I met her the last time." He noticed her being quiet and a bit dull. He thought, "How come I did not do anything about it? I assumed that she must be tired because of taking care of the child and the uncertainty of the wait in coming to live with me. How insensitive and irresponsible I was! She must have been so lonely in Ganapavaram. She stayed for days together without me and with her in-laws. She should have perhaps returned to Kalavakur instead. She might have lived with greater freedom. How come I never thought about these things? I was so engrossed in my work. After the marriage, any girl would expect to go to her husband's house and be with him, not stay at her mother's place or with in-laws. I was just focusing on my goals and responsibilities and did not think that her well-being was also my responsibility. I did not see her for almost a year! What have I done? God, please help me. I need to take good care of my wife now; hope she recovers soon." and he wondered what must have happened.

When he reached Vijayawada, he went directly to see Gurunatha Rao. As soon as Kodandaramayya entered, he said reassuringly, "Oh, good you are here. Satyam is better. Let's go to the hospital right away. Your father brought her here, and we sent someone to Kalavakur to inform Satyavathi's parent, and her family has also arrived. Kodandaramayya then said nervously, "All that is fine, but please tell me how she is now. Why is she in the hospital? Are things that bad?"

Gurunatha Rao said, "She was unconscious for two days. They brought her here yesterday, and we sent you the telegram. It looks like after dinner a couple of days ago, Satyavathi and the girls locked their door and went to sleep. In the early hours, your mother knocked on their door and saw Satyavathi lying on the floor, unresponsive. Through the window, she called the girls, who unlocked the door. When they tried to awaken Satyavathi, she was unconscious. They immediately brought her here, and I sent someone to call her family, who are all here. Now the doctor is trying to revive her."

They took a rickshaw to the hospital, and when they reached, they saw her family looking deeply concerned. As soon as they saw Kodandaramayya, they rushed to him. Sriramulu said, "You have come, let me take you to her." Kodandaramayya followed him without a word. As they were walking to the room, her doctor, Dr. Achamamaba, arrived and noticed Kodandaramayya accompanied by Sriramulu and guessed that he was Satyavathi's husband.

She came closer and, looking at Kodandaramayya, she said, "Are you Satyavathi's husband?" Kodandaramayya nodded in response. The doctor said, "She needs to return to consciousness soon. It has been two days now. Be with her, talk to her, and do whatever you can to revive her", saying this she walked away.

Kodandaramayya quickly went to Satyavathi, sat on her bed, and said, "Satyam, I am here, look" and started talking to her. His mother-in-law brought their daughter Parvathi, and the nurse said to place the baby next to her and let her call her. They put Parvathi next to her, and she called to her mother, but nothing happened. Kodandaramayya continued talking to her. The doctor walked in and said, "Satyavathi, here is your daughter. She is crying for you. Come give a kiss to your baby; she is missing you." Nothing happened. The doctor looked worried and, looking at Kodandaramayya, said, "Try, try hard," and left.

Kodandaramayya did not leave her side. While the rest of the people were waiting in the veranda, Kodandaramayya tried talking to her. He saw Satyavathi blinking her eyes and just moving her lips. He then put his hand in her mouth, and Satyavathi bit on his finger. Kodandaramayya felt hopeful that there was some response. He then tried waking her up by calling her name continuously. Satyavathi suddenly started crying, and then she finally opened her eyes. She saw her husband and she could not stop crying. Then she cried more and more; the nurse ran and called the doctor. The doctor came and held Satyavathi's hand and just let her cry. After a while, she calmed down and looked at Kodandaramayya and said, "Where am I? How come you are here? I thought you are in Madras."

Kodandaramayya said, "Yes, I am here. I have been here for the past couple of days. I came to see you when I heard that you were unwell." She smiled and then closed her eyes. Everyone, including the doctor, let out a sigh of relief.

Kodandaramayya was then called outside by the doctor. She said, "I think this has been a case of postpartum depression. This happens after delivery. Apart from that, as she has been away from you for so long, she has been missing you. It is important that you do not leave her anymore. Did you see?! You are the one who could revive her. She felt your presence. All the emotions that she has been keeping inside came out after pregnancy. Take good care of her. She is a bit delicate, both physically and emotionally. You can take her home after two days. Let us see how she progresses, and we will monitor her carefully."

Kodandaramayya nodded his head in agreement, wondering at the sudden turn of events. When Satyavathi was discharged from the hospital, her mother asked Kodandaramayya if she could take her to Kalavakur. Kodandaramayya said, "Yes, I myself was thinking that." But, Satyavathi refused and said, "I have just come here a few days ago. I am fine now. I have been there in Kalavakur for almost a year."

She was emphatic, and no one could argue with her and did not want to aggravate her condition further. Kodandaramayya assured his mother-in-law, saying, "I will be here for a few more days, don't worry, whenever she wants she will come. I will be with her." Satyavathi's parents left reluctantly.

Kodandaramayya, along with his father, Satyavathi and their daughter, went to Ganapavaram. Kodandaramayya asked her again in private, "Please think about it. If you feel more comfortable going to Kalavakur, I will come along and drop you." She said, "There is no need, I will stay in here. I have spent a long time in Kalavakur, and this way you can spend some time with your parents." Kodandaramayya's heart melted listening to this. He said, "I will go and look for a house for us and take you with me. Please be brave and take care of yourself."

He left after two days for Madras. The first time he experienced a different feeling. Whenever he left for his studies before, it was always with a determination to work hard and secure his future. This time, it was different. There was some sort of an unknown worry. He wondered how his wife would be! He questioned himself on whether or not he was doing his duty toward her.

While he was traveling, he thought, 'It is enough; now I have been expecting too much from my wife. I was just thinking about my own pursuits and goals. I have to consider my wife when I make any decisions. She is a part of my life now. I have to be mindful of that.' After reaching Madras, Kodandaramayya, with the help of his friends, tried looking for accommodation. He was living in a single room with a bathroom in a small backyard. He thought, 'How can I bring my wife here? There is no separate kitchen either. It will be too hard for us to live here with the child.'

He kept looking but could not find anything with reasonable rent that he could afford.

He was also very busy with work. Two months passed, and in Ganapavaram, Satyavathi had another attack. She was rushed to the hospital again, but the recovery was quick this time. The doctor was annoyed and said, "This is enough, please ask her husband to come and take her immediately."

Sriramulu wrote to his son asking if he could find a house and when he will be coming home next. He also wrote, "Don't worry, we are all fine here, and whenever you have time, do come." Seeing the letter, he got a bit uncomfortable and a little upset. He thought something was not right; the tone of the letter was not typical of the way his father would write. Father is always frank and open. He thought, "I better go once and see if everything is ok." On a weekend, he went to Ganapavaram. Satyavathi was looking a bit weak and pale. When Kodandaramayya asked her, she said she was fine.

After lunch, Sriramulu told his son that Satyavathi had another attack and that they had to rush her to the hospital again. He also told him that the doctor strongly advised that she should be with her husband. Sriramulu said, "Nayana, please take Satyam with you now."

Kodandaramayya asked, "Why did you not inform me?" His father responded, saying, "I did not want to worry you. Anyway, you said that you will be coming soon." This was the first time Kodandaramayya got angry at his parents. He thought, 'They are only thinking about me! What about Satyavathi? What if something serious happened?'

When he was alone with Satyavathi, Kodandaramayya asked her. She said, "Yes, I was unwell. Your parents said that you will be coming soon. Why to worry you? I also thought, maybe it is true, why to worry you? I wished you would have been there with me."

Then Kodandaramayya said, "Why was I not informed immediately?" She said, "Yes, I wanted to tell you, but how can I?" Then Kodandaramayya thought, 'Yes, how can she? It was customary that only the elders were writing letters and corresponding.' The husband and wife never corresponded with each other personally. That was not done at that time. She had borne enough so long. I am a father and a husband now. My wife has waited patiently for me. I cannot extend this anymore.

With his eldest daughter Parvathi

With his Children

Kodandaramayya with his wife Satyavathi, daughters Sri Lakshmi and Parvathi

With Children and Grand children

Chapter 8
HOUSEHOLDER

Kodandaramayya decided instantly, 'I will take my wife along with me. We will manage somehow.' He told Satyavathi, "We will go back to Madras together now. I will not leave you alone. I live in one room. You will have to adjust."

Satyavathi was worried. She was thinking about what her in-laws would say. When she expressed her worries, Kodandaramayya said, "Don't worry about it. I will take care of it. We will stay in the room where I am staying for now. We can look around for suitable accommodation from there. If you are there with me, I'd have some support too. I will tell my parents tomorrow."

Satyavathi said, "Please don't do anything in haste. I will be fine. I will never ask anything that will inconvenience you. I don't want your parents worrying about how we will manage." Kodandaramayya said, "Don't worry about it. I already told you that I would take care of it."

The next day, as soon as he woke up, he went to his father and said, "Nanna, I will have to leave in two days, and I will take Satyam with me." Just as he was saying this, Subbamma came in and heard Kodandaramayya. She said, "How will you manage there with a little child without any prior preparations? It is customary for the daughter-in-law to be accompanied by her mother or mother-in-law when she first goes to her husband's house."

Kodandaramayya smiled and said, "It's true, but she has been married for 5 years. This is not the first time she is going to her in-laws' house since she got married. She is not a new bride now. Moreover, her health is not good, and the doctor has strongly recommended that I take her with me. We will figure out other things after going there." Turning toward Sriramulu, he said, "Nanna, can you check the calendar and find a good date in the next two days for us to travel?"

Everyone sensed finality in his words. Sriramulu nodded and went inside to look at the calendar. Subbamma quietly went to talk to her daughter-in-law. She said, "Nayana wants to take you. Is it okay? Do you think you will be able to manage in a new place with a child alone? Do you think one of us should come along with you?"

Satyavathi didn't answer immediately. She did not know what to say and how her mother-in-law would react. She quietly looked at her and nodded her head. Subbamma, understood and said, "Anyway, it is your decision. I was only worried about your welfare. Now get ready for your travel," and left.

Sriramulu said to Kodandaramayya, "Day after tomorrow seems to be a good day. You can leave in the first bus."

The household started the preparations for them to leave. Subbamma packed some essential vessels and some food grains so that they did not have to go and buy everything immediately. Kodandaramayya wrote to his father-in-law that he was taking Satyavathi with him. Satyavathi thought it was unbelievable to hear that 'I am going with my husband to my own house.' She never questioned her husband about how and where they would stay, going suddenly without any preparation. None of these questions occurred to her. She just thought, 'Okay, I am going to Madras with my husband and will live there with him. Finally, I get to live where I am supposed to be.'

Kodandaramayya felt a bit bad and was thinking, 'Have I been rash and hurt my parents with this decision?' He hoped he did not. But he thought, 'What choice do I have? If Satyam gets sick again, what can I do? I am trying my best to do the right thing. They always told me to not let anyone down, myself or anyone. It was my father who taught me this. I am sure he will understand.' He went to his wife to tell her that he informed his parents and that they had agreed. Satyavathi said, "Yes, my mother-in-law told me."

Kodandaramayya thought, 'Oh, Amma must be the one who would feel a bit concerned. How come I missed that? I should have personally sat with her and spoken to her.'

He went to look for his mother who was in the backyard picking vegetables. The drumstick tree yielded so much that the tree bent down with the weight. All the green chili plants too were full of chillies. Subbamma was plucking the chillies. Kodandaramayya took the basket from her mother's hands and said, "Amma, let me do this."

Looking at her, he said, "Nanna saw the calendar and said the day after tomorrow is good for us to leave. We will leave in the morning. Don't worry, we will manage. I know you are worried about how we will manage with the little girl alone."

He looked searchingly at her face and again said, "I should probably have discussed this with you, but I took this decision very quickly."

She looked at her son and said, "Why not? I am relieved that your wife will be with you finally." She had a slight edge to her voice, "I was only a bit surprised as you had taken this decision very suddenly. Normally, you always discuss these things with us."

After saying that, she felt relieved. Kodandaramayya smiled and said, "I know, Amma, but I am also disturbed that she was unwell again. It is such a bothersome and worrisome thing for you as well. It is my fault that I have brought it to this stage. You did tell me repeatedly that I should not leave her. I did not listen to you, and this is what has happened. I was concentrating only on my work. I wanted to settle down soon and take care of the family. I thought that this is the right thing to do. I thought she would be fine living with her parents or here. I should have listened to you. You have so much more experience."

Subbamma immediately said, "Don't worry. You have done what you thought was right, and you thought about the family. Now let us get things ready for your travel. Enough talking, let me go bathe and start cooking. It is already very late. Your father will start his saga if the food is not ready on time." She hurried inside. Kodandaramayya looked at her and thought, 'It's high time my father stopped getting angry and yelling at her.'

On the day of their departure, the whole family got up early. Everyone, including the girls, got busy getting ready for their travels. Kodandaramayya and Satyavathi left for Vijayawada. The girls were very sad, especially Sita, as she watched her little niece leave. Subbamma said,"Write to us as soon as you reach."

Satyavathi sat in the train for the first time. Many thoughts flew through her head as she had these new experiences. She was a bit worried about what her in-laws were thinking. 'Were they upset? Did they think that she forced her husband to take her?' But again, she thought, 'The important thing is that I am with my husband, and it is normal for any girl to want to be with her husband. If people thought differently, then I cannot do much about it.'

They reached Madras and arrived at Kodandaramayya's room. The landlady was surprised to see Satyavathi and her daughter along with Kodandaramayya, but welcomed them anyway and gave the room key without saying anything. Satyavathi entered the house and looked around. She saw a rolled mattress on one side, some books on a mat, a water pot, and a couple of glasses next to it. It had the complete air of a bachelor's room. There was a door leading to the backyard. Kodandaramayya walked through it and showed her where the bathroom and toilet were. He told her to go and take a bath, and then they would go out and eat in the mess where he ate regularly. He said, "While coming back, we will bring the essential things we need. Now I will go and talk to the landlady and explain to her about your sudden arrival."

When he left, Satyavathi started unpacking. She opened the 2 bags containing the vessels and groceries. Kodandaramayya came back and began to help her. The landlady walked in and said, "You should have your meals with us today. After some rest, you can start cooking your meals from tomorrow."

When she saw the couple hesitate, she insisted. The next day, Kodandaramayya went out and bought some vegetables and other essential groceries. Satyavathi started to cook rice. She noticed that the rice was not cooking, no matter how much water she added.

She initially didn't understand what was happening, so she went to talk to the landlady. When Satyavathi said, "I have been cooking the rice for so long, I don't understand why it won't cook."

The landlady smiled and thought, 'Oh, the young girl starting her family.' She said, "Let me come and see."

When she saw the rice, she said, "Oh, this is not normal rice. This is parboiled rice. Here, many people eat parboiled rice. You should ask for Pachi Arisi, which is raw rice. Boiled rice takes a very long time to cook. It will at least take an hour or 2 to cook; normally, this rice is cooked on firewood, not on a small stove like this. If you cook it on a small stove like this, it will take forever. You don't find this rice in Andhra Pradesh. For now, let it be. Leave it on the stove; it will take a long time but, once done, the taste is not bad; one should get used to it. Tell Kodandaramayya to ask for raw rice. Keep this rice, and you can use it for idly and dosa."

Later in life, whenever they were going through financially hard times, Satyavathi would think, "We started our journey as a family with boiled rice, which takes forever to cook. That's why I am facing these challenges."

After a month, they found a small portion of a house with two rooms, a kitchen, and a small back veranda. They rented it out from Ogirala Ramachandrudu, who was a famous music director, whom Kodanda knew earlier. They were also a Telugu-speaking family from Andhra. Kodandaramayya was back to his old work habits, and Satyavathi handled everything in the house. Some evenings, when Kodandaramayya came home a bit early, he would take them to Marina beach. Sometimes they would go to Kapaleswara temple.

Satyavathi wrote to her family that all was well and that they need not worry about her. Everyone at Kalavakur was happy and felt relieved, when they received this news from her. A few months passed by, and they received a letter that Sakuntala, Satyavathi's sister-in-law, was unwell and that she has to undergo some sort of surgery. The letter said that it should be done in Madras, as the hospitals there are advanced and better. Sakuntala, along with Satyavathi's brother and her nephew, came to Madras. Satyavathi was happy to see them, though she was worried for her sister-in-law. They stayed on for a few days, and after successfully getting the surgery done and when Sakuntala was ready to travel, they left. The thought of how they could accommodate guests in that small place never occurred to them. They all adjusted, and everything went well.

The announcement finally was made that the High Court would be moving to Guntur. All the Telugu-speaking people who wanted to move to Andhra Pradesh started preparations.

Mr. Venkatesam also decided to move to the Andhra Pradesh High Court.

Kodandaramayya told Satyavathi about the move. He further added, "I will have to find a school for both my sisters. I have to also spend a lot of time with my senior, as we are moving the office to Guntur. We need to look into a lot of official things. It will be difficult for you to manage alone, as I will be coming home at odd times. I will have to help my senior in winding up the office here and setting up the office in Guntur. Then, I have to find a house for us close to the office so that my commute is easier. Once all this is settled, I will bring both my sisters and join them in the school. They are suffering without proper education in Ganapavaram. Education is very important these days. As soon as these things are settled, I will call you. I can vacate this house and share accommodation with a friend so we can save some money."

Satyavathi said, "Whatever is convenient, we will do that. Let us go to Ganapavaram first. Someone will come from Kalavakur and take me later to Kalavakur." After living with her husband, there had arisen in her a newfound peace and confidence.

That settled, they got into their routine. A couple of days before their departure, they went to Kapaleswara temple and the beach, which they both enjoyed very much. Kodandaramayya thought, "I have lived in Visakhapatnam and Madras, both are cities by the sea. I am going to miss the oceanside. I always used to come here regularly, and it gave me such joy."

They went and met the acquaintances they had made in Madras and bid farewell. Kodandaramayya also wrote to his father-in-law about the move, mentioning that whenever convenient, Satyavathi would travel to Kalavakur.

They packed up their small household and headed to Ganapavaram. At home, everyone felt joyful that

Kodandaramayya would move to Guntur, which is much closer than Madras. He left after a couple of days, telling his parents that he had to help his senior who is arriving at Guntur to look for the office. He also said that as soon as he finds a house, he will take his sisters and enrol them in school. He said that it is important he does these things quickly.

Both the parents felt a kind of satisfaction and at peace that finally they were seeing the fruits of their hard work. His mother looked at her son and said, "Nayana, whatever you think is best, do it. Now everything is in your hands; all the burden is on your shoulders."

Kodandaramayya said, "Amma, don't worry about all this. I have to do these things. Taking care of the family is not a burden; that is what we are supposed to do. What else is one to do?"

Kodandaramayya's notion of family began with his parents and his sisters, now his wife and daughter. After Kodandaramayya left, Satyavathi stayed on for almost 3 weeks, and then her brother came and took her to Kalavakur. Less than a month later, Kodandaramayya wrote to his father that he found a house in Guntur and that he will come and take his sisters first because the new academic year is starting, and that he had to enrol the girls in school and college immediately.

Sita, the younger sister, was elated. She thought, 'Finally, my dream is coming true. I always wanted to go and study in a proper school.' The older sister had her own apprehensions. She was unsure of how and what she was going to study and how she would adjust in a new place and in a school. 'Is it going to be a school or college?' For her age, she was not really sure. She thought, 'I never left my village. I wonder how it is going to be?'

Kodandaramayya paid an advance for the house. The landlady was very helpful. She said, "Come day after tomorrow, it's a good day. I will do the necessary pooja."

Kodandaramayya thanked her and then brought pictures of the goddesses Saraswathi and Lakshmi, and a picture of Kodandarama Swamy. All prints of the famous artist Raja Ravi Varma. He was especially fascinated by the picture of Kodandarama Swamy.

All these pictures went with him and adorned every home he lived in. He entered the house with these pictures. He walked to the office every day, and then he would go to the court with his senior, Mr. Venkatesam, and come home around 7 or 8 P.M at night after finishing his work in the office.

Summer holidays came to an end. Schools announced reopening dates. Kodandaramayya went to Ganapavaram and brought both his sisters with him to Guntur. Sita, his younger sister was enrolled into middle school and Venkayamma, the older one into an institute to appear privately for her matriculation exams. A month later, Satyavathi also joined them. Kodandaramayya felt, 'Now I am a full-fledged family man running a household.' He smiled to himself. Whenever possible, he would send small amounts of money to his parents. Sriramulu wrote to him saying, "Nayana, mother, and I will manage somehow; the whole family is with you. Don't worry about sending me money."

But Kodandaramayya, smiling to himself, thought, 'My father is ever considerate and always thinks of my welfare. He is getting old, his energy has reduced. His earnings are almost diminished. How will he manage? He is such a proud man.'

Mr. Venkatesam took on two more juniors and office clerks into his legal practice . His office was now a full-fledged senior advocate's office. Kodandaramayya was also very happy that he found a real guru in Mr. Venkatesam. He plunged into his work and assiduously applied himself to his professional growth.

Two years passed uneventfully, except for Venkayamma lack of interest in her studies and continuously failed in her matriculation twice in a row. Kodandaramayya did not give up. He exhorted , "You have to have a high school certificate or something equal . One will never know when this education will come in handy. Work hard somehow and complete matriculation." His parents said, "Nayana, this girl has no interest in studies. Why are you forcing her? Let us find an appropriate match and get her married. Why are you wasting your time, money, and energy."

Her sister, too, thought, 'Why is Annayya so keen on making me study? I know Telugu. I can read and write well. I can manage a family with the education I have.'

Kodandaramayya said, "Minimum education is important, Nanna. Instead of encouraging her, why are you discouraging her? Education will never go to waste. Please help her."

And he also told his younger sister, "Why don't you help Akka in her studies? She has to, at least, pass matriculation."

Looking at her older sister, to encourage her, he said, "Look at Sita, how deeply she is interested in studies. She will surely get a degree."

None of these things entered her head. She simply didn't want to study. She thought 'I am trying to put my mind into it, but I am not able to grasp anything. This means I am not the person to have an education. Maybe I have no mind for academics.' In the end she did complete her matriculation. Kodandaramayya's perseverance proved right later in her life when Vekayamma procured a job to teach adults on basis that she has appeared for the Metriculation exam.

Kodandaramayya made sure that the family did not miss out on the small pleasures of life. Once, when he heard his sisters and his wife discussing a famous Hindi movie, 'Jhanak Jhanak Payal Baje,' and his younger sister was saying that her friend from school had seen it and it was just amazing, Kodandaramayya went to them and said, "Why don't you all go tomorrow and watch the movie?"

Sita thought, 'My God! Annayya heard me talking about movies. I hope he won't be upset at it.' But that didn't happen. Kodandaramayya said, "Go tomorrow, finish your work quickly and go to the first show. I have a lot of work at the office. Anyway, by the time I come home, it will be late, and you will be back by then." Since then, the family watched movies once in a while. They always brought jasmine flowers in summer. In South India, women loved to adorn their hair with jasmine flowers. Whenever possible, he would buy new clothes for the festivals for his sisters and daughter, if not for his wife. When his daughter was 2 years old, Satyavathi was pregnant again. Her mother came and took her to Kalavakur for the delivery in the fifth month of her pregnancy. She performed Srimantham, the baby shower, for which Subbamma also came to attend the function. She had never come to Guntur before. Taking this opportunity, she also came and saw her son's household. She then stayed for a month to cook for her daughters and Kodandaramayya. Soon enough, Satyavathi delivered a healthy baby boy to everyone's delight. Sriramulu was thrilled that he had a grandson.

Things were changing in the country. Hyderabad was chosen to be the new capital city of Andhra Pradesh. Preparations started for the High Court to move to Hyderabad. A magnificent building, constructed by the seventh Nizam of Hyderabad, Mir Usman Ali Khan, was chosen to house the High Court of Andhra Pradesh under the State Recognition Act. It was inaugurated on November 5th, 1956.

Mr. Venkatesam decided to move to Hyderabad to set up his practice in the High Court. Summer holidays had begun, and the girls went to Ganapavaram.

Kodandaramayya went to Kalavakur to see his son and to perform the naming ceremony. He named his son "Sri Raghuram." This time, Sriramulu, Subbamma, and the girls also came to Kalavakur for the function. After spending a couple of days there, Kodandaramayya returned to Guntur, informing Satyavathi that he would move to Hyderabad soon. He planned to take her to Hyderabad as soon as he found a suitable home for rent.

Chapter 9
SETTLING INTO THE PROFESSION

Kodandaramayya moved to Hyderabad along with Mr. Venkatesam and his other colleagues. He found a room with a small kitchen and got busy setting up the office. As soon as the schools opened, Kodandaramayya went and brought his younger sister Sita and enrolled her at the highly reputed Stanley Girl's High School. He came to know about the school through one of his neighbours who was a Telugu pandit in that school. Sita, of course, was overjoyed that she was going to a fancy English medium school. This was her dream come true. She thanked her brother in her heart a million times.

It took almost 3 months for Kodandaramayya to find a house where he could set up his family. He found a house in Nampally near the Hyderabad railway station at Pattar Masjid. It was walking distance to Sita's school and almost 6 kilometres to Kodandaramayya's office. Satyavathi and the children came along with his elder sister, Venkayyamma, after 6 months. He enrolled his daughter Parvathi in the same school as Sita.

Kodandaramayya would walk to his office every morning and go to the High Court from there along with his senior, Mr. Venkatesam, and his colleagues. They would walk all the way and be back in the evening at the office. Kodandaramayya would then stay there until he finished all his office work and then go back home on foot. Walking, walking, and walking. Walking had become a way of life for him. He always walked wherever he went. Somehow, he never got into the practice of getting onto a city bus. Either he walked or he took a rickshaw when it was too far or when he was very tired. Even as he was learning the ropes as a junior advocate, he displayed enough discipline to engage in a range of academic writings in law. In one of his articles, he suggested empowering the district courts with the constitutional power to issue writs for enforcing fundamental rights. This dynamic interpretation of the Constitution has gained relevance over the years, given the increasing difficulty in accessing justice.

Mr. Venkatesam suggested to Adinarayana Raju and Kodandaramayya, both his juniors, to write a book on Tenancy Laws of Andhra Pradesh. Of course, both the colleagues took the task very seriously right away and worked on it. Now, this took a lot of time. By the time Kodandaramayya reached home after working on the book, it was almost 9 o'clock in the night. Again, the next morning he would leave home by 8 a.m. This went on for almost a year. In the end, they successfully completed the book and got it published.

Satyavathi always waited for him to come home. She ate only after serving his meal. By the time Kodandaramayya reached home, most of the time, children would be asleep; only his younger sister would be awake, studying. Kodandaramayya used to feel happy seeing his sister's interest in studies.

The couple were blessed with another daughter. Kodandaramayya named her Sri Lakshmi. He said to his wife, "We have Parvathi; now Lakshmi has come to our house." Satyavathi always said that for the first time, they bought a 50-kilo sack of rice after Lakshmi was born.

Whenever Kodandaramayya had some time, he would walk to Sitarambagh, a very old Sri Rama temple which was almost 5 km from their house. Kodandaramayya's spiritual sadhana started from this point onwards. He became an ardent bhaktha of

Sri Rama. Sri Rama was, in fact, their family deity. He bought a copy of Valmiki Ramayana and approached a teacher who would come home whenever Kodandaramayya had some free time and explained the epic to him.

It was getting difficult for Kodandaramayya to commute from Nampally to Himayathnagar. He felt that a lot of time was being wasted. He could use that time in better ways than in commuting. He decided to move to Himayathnagar, where his office was located. Mr. Venkatesam's residence was also there. Moreover, Himayathnagar was considered a good locality, where mostly professionals lived. Within a few days, he found a four-room flat right on the main road. Traffic was not a problem in those days. The place was centrally located. Everything was within walking distance. Kodandaramayya moved with his family there. Sita, his younger sister, and Parvathi, his daughter, would take a bus to their school, which was in Abids.

Kodandaramayya's spiritual interests began to grow. His work, his family, and his spiritual sadhana and swadhyayana (Self-study) took up all his time. During this time, Kodandaramayya used to attend Sri Chinmayananda's lectures regularly.

The pressure from his parents to perform the marriage of their elder daughter, Venkayamma had increased. She was also ready to get married. Finally, Kodandaramayya also got convinced that if she is not interested in studying further, there was no point in forcing her. He told his parents to go ahead and look for alliances.

Gurunatha Rao, his cousin who was older than Kodandaramayya, got married to a doctor from Hyderabad, Dr. Vijayalakshmi. Her family became very close to Kodandaramayya and his wife. Dr. Vijayalakshmi's father, Sri Jagannatha Sastry, a well-read and spiritual man, was a great devotee of Sri Krishna. Kodandaramayya instantly took to him. He often visited him in the evenings whenever he had some time. Jagannatha Sastry became his first guru. Kodandaramayya studied Bhagavad-Gita with him. Jagannatha Sastry also developed great affection toward Kodandaramayya.

Dr Vijayalakshmi's family lived in Barkathpura, which was not far from Himayathnagar. Both families became very close, as Vijayalakshmi's mother treated Satyavathi as her daughter. Dr Vijayalakshmi had two other sisters, the younger of whom was also a doctor. She had two younger brothers who were academic geniuses. Their mother, a divine lady, extended help to all those around her. Dr Vijayalakshmi's younger brother became a renowned doctor. Her older brother was an army officer. Once Vijayalakshmi came into the family, she became a guardian angel for Satyavathi and the family. She ensured that all the medical needs of the family were met. She too developed great affection toward the family and treated the children like her own. Both families always supported each other. The love and friendship that Gurunatha Rao and Kodandaramayya had for each other was extended to their families as well.

The parents found a groom for Venkayyamma. The groom was married before, and his wife passed away in childbirth. The child from the groom's first marriage was three years old when this alliance was proposed. Sriramulu visited the family of the groom and noted that the family had large property and also had Karanikam (hereditarily the family member becomes head of the village). Sriramulu was satisfied and asked Kodandaramayya to come to Ganapavaram to discuss the marriage arrangements. When Kodandaramayya went to Ganapavaram, he said, "I went and saw their house. They have lands, and the family is well respected. Yes, the boy was married once and also has a child. However, I don't think we can get a better match. He is also very good looking and a handsome boy. He has three older brothers. He does not have many responsibilities. His eldest brother runs the show. Let us go ahead and fix this alliance."

Kodandaramayya felt rather uncertain. He went to his sister and said, "Amma, think about this; you are never a burden for me. We can wait and look for other matches. Unless you are completely convinced, there is no need to accept this alliance. Think carefully, as there is also a child involved, and we are in no hurry, we can wait. Meanwhile, you can complete your matriculation. Think about it and let me know."

He told his parents not to make a hasty decision. He said, "It's a question of her life. I will have to go back to Hyderabad. Please think about all aspects carefully and let me know."

A week later, he received a letter from his father stating that they had decided to proceed with the proposal and that everyone was in agreement. Quietly, father and son managed the finances and performed the marriage ceremony as best as they could. Kodandaramayya made sure that the groom's family had no complaints. All the relatives who attended the marriage were given appropriate gifts. Venkayyamma wondered, 'How did my brother manage all this?' She touched his feet with tears in her eyes and took his blessings before leaving for her new house. Within a year, Kodandaramayya repaid all the debts he had taken for the marriage. The family members never knew how he managed the finances for the marriage or how he paid off the debts.

Satyavathi fell ill a few months after the marriage of her sister-in-law. Initially, they thought that she was tired after the wedding preparations, and that it would settle. However, she developed severe stomach ache that persisted. They visited the family doctor, but even after taking the medicines, the pain persisted. The doctor suggested that she should be admitted into the Osmania General Hospital for relevant tests. She stayed in the hospital for almost 3 months, but the doctors could not find anything serious. Subbamma came to stay with them. Sita had completed her pre-university course by then and went to live in Ganapavaram with her father.

Whatever the situation, Kodandaramayya never lost his composure. At every stage, he showed his wisdom and was never perturbed by any eventualities. His wife was in the hospital, and 3 children were at home with his mother. He managed everything at home along with his career. The youngest daughter, Sri Lakshmi, was three years old. His mother, Subbamma, was a pillar of support.

When he was going to the court in the morning, he would take food for his wife to the Osmania Hospital, which is right opposite the High Court. In the evening, whenever he had time, he would go and visit his wife, stay with her for some time, and then go home. This went on for almost three months. The ever-patient Satyavathi ate her lunch which her husband brought before going to court and saved some food for dinner. She ate the same cold food without a word of complaint. Kodandaramayya used to feel bad but could not do much about it. As the hospital was very far from the house, going a second time was impossible. He had no other help.

Kodandaramayya never once got frustrated, nor was upset with anyone. He thought that things happen the way they were meant to happen and went with the flow without complaining. Doctors could not find anything wrong with Satyavathi, but she had pain and she suffered. Finally, they decided that she needed good rest and needed to be looked after for some time. Satyavathi got discharged and went to Kalavakur, stayed there for a couple of months, got better, and then returned to Hyderabad.

Senior Advocate, Kodandaramayya and his Colleagues

Colleagues Krishnam Raju and Adinarayana Raju

Chapter 10
GROWING PERSONALLY AND PROFESSIONALLY

Mr. Venkatesam, his senior and guru, was elevated to the bench. It was a great honour and pleasure for his entire office. He admired Mr. Venkatesam for his uprightness, the way he developed his practice, and his knowledge.

Mr. Venkatesam, in turn, was impressed by Kodandaramayya's sincerity, hard work, and chivalry. By then, Venkatesam's son, Mr. Bhagiratha Rao, was also enrolled at the bar and joined the practice. He excelled as a criminal lawyer. Apart from Kodandaramayya, Aadinarayana Raju, Krishnan Raju, Venkat Raju, and Sathyanarayana Rao were all juniors of Mr. Venkatesam. Sri Gopalam was the office clerk, a hardworking and sincere person; he gained great respect from everybody in the office.

After Mr. Venkatesam became the justice of the High Court of Andhra Pradesh, he handed over the office to Kodandaramayya. Kodandaramayya became a senior advocate. Mr. Venkatesam's son, Bhagiratha Rao, also joined Kodandaramayya's office and continued to work with him. Kodandaramayya moved to a new place where he could accommodate both his residence and the office. His work and his personal sadhana began to grow in tandem.

Somehow, a thought crossed his mind to have a second son. Soon, his wish came true. The couple were blessed with another son. Satyavathi delivered the child in Hyderabad without going to her parents' place as per the custom. Her mother came to help her. Kodandaramayya performed the naming ceremony and called his second son Kasi Viswanath. He thought, "I wanted a second son, Shiva has blessed me." Kodandaramayya celebrated the naming ceremony of his son joyously. He never hesitated to celebrate happy occasions. Regardless of additional expenses, he did what he thought was appropriate. Balancing his career aspirations with the responsibilities of a growing family, he remained steadfast in fulfilling his familial duties and initiating and practicing his spiritual sadhana.

Around this time, his elder sister Venkayamma also became pregnant and came to Hyderabad for delivery. Again, Satyavathi and Kodandaramayya performed all the necessary rituals. She later had two other children, and both times she came to Hyderabad to deliver her children and left after staying with them for three months, as per the custom.

It never occurred to Kodandaramayya or Satyavathi whether they could afford to take on these responsibilities or not because of financial constraints. They accepted it without a second thought.

Time passed at its own pace. Kodandaramayya had a pleasant surprise. Satyavathi was pregnant again with her fifth child, and she delivered a baby boy whom Kodandaramayya named Varaha Lakshmi Narasimha. Satyavathi saw Lord Narasimha Swamy in her dream just before the delivery. The couple were very happy. They both thought, "We have to take good care of our children and bring them up properly." They somehow managed this beautifully well inspite of deep financial constraints.

Beginning from1963, Kodandaramayya spent a lot of time reading and understanding spiritual books. He would regularly attend talks by various spiritual leaders. He also started to read books by Swami Vivekananda and was greatly influenced by his teachings. He got a picture of him and hung it in the main hall.

In the pursuit of self-discovery and self-improvement, he started collecting various spiritual and literary books in Telugu and English. He used to tell his children, "One should have a good collection of classics and biographies." Some of the books he got early on were works of William Shakespeare, One Hundred Great Lives, books of Aurobindo, Swami Vivekananda, Ramakrishna Paramahamsa, 'Experiments with Truth' by Mahatma Gandhi, Rajagopalachari's Ramayana and Mahabharata, Panchatantra, not to forget the dictionaries of English and Telugu.

He also collected Telugu classics. To name a few of them - Valmiki Ramayana, Mahabharata by Vyasa, Telugu Bhagavatham, and a few other similar ones. The Prabhandas written by Ashta Diggajas, and Ramakrishna Kathamrutha were a few of those books. As time went by, slowly all the cupboards in the house started filling up with his books. Satyavathi would get frustrated and say, "Can you leave some place for me? Where am I supposed to keep all the household things?" He would smile and say, "This is the only wealth I have."

Sri Viswanatha Saryanarayana, a renowned Telugu poet, scholar, and novelist, who was a Padmabushan and Gnanapeeth awardee, was Kodandaramayya's teacher when he was in college. He was also a close friend of Gurunatha Rao. Whenever Kodandaramayya went to Vijayawada, he would meet Sri Satyanarayana, who was a great devotee of Sri Rama and wrote a version of the Ramayanam, the "Ramayana Kalpavriksham."

Kodandaramayya used to have long chats with him on various literary and spiritual topics. During one of those meetings, he asked Sri Satyanarayana how he became such an ardent devotee of Sri Rama. After listening to the great poet, he got inspired and requested Sri Satyanarayana to write a book on that topic in poetic form, and that he would publish it. Satyanarayana accepted and wrote beautiful verses about Sri Rama and his devotion. The book was called Na Ramudu (My Rama).

He took an organized trip with Chinmaya Mission to Bhadrachalam. When he visited Bhadrachalam, apart from visiting the main temple of Sri Rama, he also went to Amba Satram, which was founded by Pamidighantam Venkataramana Das, a great devotee of Sri Rama. This was also included in the pilgrimage.

The story goes that a great siddha purusha (enlightened soul) came from North India and gave Sri Venkataramana Das the statues of goddess Durga, Sri Rama, Lakshmana, Sita, and Hanuman. He said that Devi came in his dream and asked him to hand over all these to Venkataramana Das. Venkataramana Das accepted this as the order of Devi and established the statues, performed appropriate rituals and pujas regularly, and named the place as Amba Satram. (Satram: A place where one can eat and sleep free or for a minimum price while traveling or on a pilgrimage.)

In the Satram, they showed him two huge brass vessels in which they used to cook rice for Annadanam. No one could move them from the big firewood stove after the rice was cooked. Only when Venkataramana Das came and touched the vessel, it would move. They also showed him a small grinding stone and said Venkataramana Das would sit in front of it and make chutney. No matter how many hundreds of pilgrims came for the meal, he would keep filling the serving dishes, and chutney kept coming till the last person was served. A number of such anecdotes were told about Venkataramana Das. Many people used to say that they felt Devi Durga's presence in the Satram. Also, Sri Rama and Lakshmana came to the aid of Venkataramana Das a number of times when he was in need.

The Satram was in a dilapidated state when Kodandaramayya visited it. Though Venkataramana Das donated all his property to the Satram, which was a good number of acres. After he passed away, the property fell into a state of neglect. The lands bequeathed to the Satram were illegally occupied, and no income was forthcoming to maintain the establishment.

Kodandaramayya was touched by hearing the story of Venkataramana Das. When he came home, he wrote to his father inquiring about Venkataramana Das and Amba Satram. His father immediately replied, saying that Venkataramana Das is Kodandaramayya's aunt's (his mother's sister) father-in-law's brother, who is also a Pamidighantam and was a great devotee of Sri Rama. He also added that Venkataramana Das was unmarried and devoted his life to Sri Rama. He had a lot of property, all of which he gave to the Satram. They are fortunate to have such a person in their family.

Now, Kodandaramayya got fully convinced that he could not let this great place fall to neglect. He almost felt that it was his duty to revive it, as he is of Pamidighantam descent and a devotee of Sri Rama. Those days, people of the same family name felt close to each other and felt a kind of responsibility toward each other. He took up the project at a later time and brought it back to its glory. From then, he regularly visited Bhadrachalam. He tried hard and got back as much of the property as he could to the Satram, from people who occupied it, and handed it over to Sringeri Sankar Muth to run it.

Every day, after coming back home from the court, he would wash up and rest for 15 or 20 minutes. While he was resting, children would sit around, and he would chat with them. He would then go into his office and look into his matters for the next day, for almost a couple of hours or more, he would apply himself to the preparatory work. He found great pleasure in academic reading; apart from reading journals, he extensively read legal texts and books by eminent authors.

Around this time, Kodandaramayya used to undertake pilgrimages. He hardly went on holiday or sightseeing; his travels were always to holy places. It is the holy shrines that he was interested in. During one such trip, he went to North India, planning to cover many places. Kodandaramayya, with his ardent quest for learning, somehow did not learn languages quickly. He was in Madras for a while, but somehow, he did not pick up Tamil well. He lived in Hyderabad and was never fluent in Hindi. He used to somehow manage a bit here and there.

When he went to North India, he said that he managed his trip with three sentences. He used to tell people, "I came from Hyderabad. I am an advocate, and I cannot speak Hindi very well." He used to say that the moment he mentioned he was a "vakil sahib," people immediately respected him and helped him. He would call home once every couple of days to let his family know where he was and also to make sure that all was well at home. He travelled up to Kashi on this trip while covering a few places in Maharashtra and Madhya Pradesh.

His parents started to look for marriage proposals for their younger daughter, Sita. They said, "It's time that we seriously think about her marriage. Once this responsibility is over, we will be relaxed."

Kodandaramayya said, "Please don't hurry like you did with my elder sister. Sita is educated, let us take time and look for something suitable."

The landlord who rented the house to Kodandaramayya was transferred to Hyderabad, and he asked Kodandaramayya to vacate the house. Kodandaramayya had no choice but to look for another accommodation.

He found one in Himayathnagar itself on road number 12 and moved there. He lived there for almost 12 years. This is where a number of important events of his life happened.

His second sister, Sita, completed high school and wanted to study BA. Those were the days when the dowry system was very prevalent. Hardly any girl got married without dowry. Depending on the education of the boy, the dowry would vary. Kodandaramayya's parents said if she completed her BA, they would have to look for a boy who would have studied MA. No man would like to marry any girl who studied more than him. The dowry would go up as per the qualifications of the groom. It was a pathetic situation for the girls and a social evil of those days. His parents said they could not afford such high dowry. Kodandaramayya was pained at this state of affairs and felt sad that he was unable to send her to college. He too knew that would be a huge financial burden and that he may not have the capacity to fulfil the need.

Though Sita was very interested in studying further, she understood the situation. He told Sita, "I understand your wish to study further. But what father is saying is also true. Why don't you appear for BA exams privately and write the exams? This way, we can avoid the college expenses, and if you find difficulty in any subject, we can engage a tutor. Your wish to study will be fulfilled without much burden."

Sita agreed and Kodandaramayya bought the necessary books and gave them to her. However, her plans did not materialize at that time. Sita did complete BA after her marriage, but only after she became a mother of 3 children.

It was always an ordeal for Kodandaramayya to send money regularly to his aging parents back home. He had been persistently asking them to move to Hyderabad, since his sister Venkayamma got married. Giving some reason or the other they kept postponing. Pressure from his parents increased to perform the marriage of his younger sister Sita. Sita has been shuttling between Ganapavarm and Hyderbad. Monetory struggle went on with his growing family and other responsibilities.

It was not his father, Sriramulu, who was resistant, but Subbamma, his mother, rejected the idea vehemently. She felt that she would lose her freedom. She thought she could live in her own house and in the village they adopted; until the end of her life. Not that she didn't trust her son, by nature she was a very independent person. She used to say a proverb in Telugu *"Svathanthram swargam, ahanthram prana sankatam,"* which means being independent is heaven, dependence is a threat to life. Her children used to make fun of her saying "amma sometimes creates her own proverbs depending on her convenience.

One day, Kodandaramayya suddenly made a decision and went to Ganapavaram. He sat his parents down and said, "You both are here living alone at this age. I am sitting in Hyderabad busy with my work and other responsibilities and constantly wondering how you both are doing here. I am unable to send money regularly on time and worry constantly whether you are able to eat well, are healthy, and generally how you are managing the household. If we are together, we eat or starve, but we are all at one place together and can be there for each other. Both of you are getting old, eventually you will have to come to Hyderabad. As you know, I will not be able to move back here. Please think about it. I will not take no for an answer. " He then left for Hyderabad, asking them to reflect seriously and come to a decision.

Sriramulu understood the situation and said to his wife, "Enough is enough. No need to trouble our son anymore, we need to move to Hyderabad."

It is not that Subamma, didn't understand the situation. Being in her own territory and in her household, she was fully independent. All that would change for her. Her daughter-in-law may not object to whatever she does, but sharing and consulting for everything is not easy. She thought so much adjustment at this age would not be easy. However, she knew in her heart of hearts that she had no choice but to leave.

She took a couple of days to come to terms with it. With great difficulty, she made her decision and told her husband, "Let's move to Hyderabad. I can see how our son is troubled, and there is no point troubling him by continuing to stay here. He is the one who will eventually take care of us, and let's do what he wishes us to do."

Sriramulu, looked at his wife and felt a pang of pain in his heart. He understood how hard this decision was for her to make, and he couldn't do anything about it. He said, "Where are we going? We are only going to our son, who unconditionally took responsibility of the family." He felt an overwhelming love and tenderness for his son. Whatever trace of sadness was present when he looked at his wife it vanished away.

Sriramulu wrote to his son that they finally took the decision to move to Hyderabad as per his wish. He also wrote, "We will be happy to be with you. Where else will we be in our old age? I will inform a few of my close acquaintances and tell them that we are selling the house. Let's see what will happen." After receiving the letter, Kodandaramayya informed his wife that his parents have finally decided to move. Satyavathi was a bit apprehensive but thought, 'What is there to think about it? Do I have a choice or say in this matter? What else can I do, except to adjust? Moreover, where else will they go? One day or other they will be here because my husband is the only son, and I have to take care of them. Maybe sooner than later. At least now they are active and are able to take care of themselves. My mother-in-law is not someone who is lazy, or sits around and makes me do all the work. It will be easy to get adjusted when they are well and active. "

Time passed, and within two months, the house was sold. Sriramulu wrote to his son and informed him that there was a buyer who asked for 3 months' time for the full payment. Kodandaramayya said, "That is good, we will have enough time to prepare. I will have summer holidays, and we can move during that time." He also thought, 'My mother will also have some time to mentally prepare for the move.'

Two months later, Sriramulu wrote to Kodandaramayya that he had to start looking for a groom for Sita. Sita was inHyderabad at that time. Kodandaramayya wrote back immediately saying, "We will do that as soon as you move here. Let us not hurry and get overwhelmed handling too many things at the same time. I will send Sita so that she can help you and amma through this period of transition. It will be nice for her also to spend some time with you in Ganapavaram. She was born and brought up in that house. I am sure she would like that"

Sriramulu and Subbamma moving to Hyderabad was a big change in everyone's lives. Interestingly, Kodandaramayya never once pondered over these changes or events as a hardship, or an obligation. For him, all these responsibilities were a natural part of his life. Everything fell into place eventually. That is because he never thought this was a burden or another responsibility added to his duties. He never thought, 'Oh! One more thing on my head!' or 'How am I going to fulfil this job?' Maybe that is the reason all through his life he did everything without a complaint or resistance. The incredible quality of Titiksha (perseverance) helped him in his life journey. There was no room for self pity in his life.

The date was set for his parents to move during the summer holidays. Something interesting happened on the day he was leaving for Ganapavaram to bring his parents. He planned to take the night train from Secunderabad.

As Secunderabad station was far from Himayathnagar, where they resided, he called for an auto. The children and Satyavathi walked up to the gate with him to bid him farewell as he got into the auto. His eldest daughter Parvathi, who was thirteen years old at the time, used to accompany him wherever he went. On that occasion, as he was getting into the auto, he looked at his daughter and said, "Parvathi! You come along with me!" Without a moment of hesitation, she got into the auto, Kodandaramayya then waved his hand, gesturing to the driver to go ahead. Satyavathi and the other children were surprised and wondered why he was taking Parvathi with him.

In the auto, Parvathi was thinking, 'Something is on his mind. Is he taking me along with him to Ganapavaram? But I have school tomorrow. I did not pack any clothes.' She didn't utter a word. She happily sat in the auto next to her father. Throughout the auto ride, her father spoke to her about how it was when they first moved to Ganapavaram and how he considered that village as his native place. He said, "If anyone asks which is your native place? you should say, 'I am from Ganapavaram, Krishna District.'" Then he went on to say, my original village is Modepally, but my father moved from there when he lost his property, and he never looked back, so I have no connection with that village," Parvathi just nodded her head, without understanding much and said, "Yes, Nanna garu."

As they were reaching the station, he looked at his daughter and asked, "You can go home safely, right? You have to be brave." She nodded her head. She was scared and afraid because she had never been to Secunderabad station, which was much bigger and farther than Nampally station, where they used to go quite often. She didn't utter a word. When they reached the station, they both walked up to the main gate and Kodandaramayya, then stopped and said, "Now you can go home," as he handed a couple of rupees and walked into the station. She thought, 'Father wanted some company, as he was going on a big mission. Maybe he was lonely and agitated.' She couldn't fully understand but felt that her father was a bit unnerved. Later in life whenever Parvathi recollected that incident, she would think "father never again showed that kind of emotion anytime, except for a moment when we lost our grandfather." At home, Satyavathi and others were panicking, wondering what had happened to Parvathi. They had no way to contact anyone. When Parvathi reached home around 10 P.M and narrated the story, Satyavathi did not know what to make of it. She was relieved that her daughter was safe at home but was upset with her husband. Parvathi felt a great sense of pride thinking that her father trusted her and thought that she is brave and capable. When she expressed this to her mother, she said, "Just keep quiet, you and your courage. God is with us and brought you home safely."

Kodandaramayya reached Ganapavaram wondering the whole time how his parents were, especially his mother. It was around 10 A.M when he entered the house, he saw his father packing a jute bag with some utensils. As soon as he saw Kodandaramayya, his face lit up. He shouted, "Nayana is here!"

Subbamma hurriedly came out and looked at Kodandaramayya affectionately. She said, "All good, Nayana. I am happy to join you and my daughter-in-law. You were right; it's time we all live together. Even the villagers were advising the same thing for a long time. They keep saying repeatedly that 'You have a loving and an efficient son who wants to take care of you; you should not resist.' They said, 'Don't have any doubts in your mind. Just go live with him.'" She continued to say, "I have no hesitation in my mind or heart. This is the right time to move in with you."

Kodandaramayya smiled at his mother, went close to her, and hugged her. He said, "Amma, I am so happy you said this! I was a bit nervous. Let us get to work!" Both parents smiled. His mother said, "First, have your bath and rest a bit. After lunch, we can see what else is to be done."

When Kodandaramayya walked to the backyard, he saw a huge pile of fire wood.. He asked Sita, who followed him, "Did father buy so much firewood? When we are moving away from here permanently? I didn't see it the last time I was here." Sita said with a kind of frustrated look, "Annayya, don't you remember? The big neem tree that fell down during the monsoon season. All this while we only used the branches as firewood. The main trunk was intact, but during summer, it dried completely. Nanna cut it himself, and now he is planning to take it to Hyderabad. I have tried explaining to him that he can't possibly move it to Hyderabad; he got angry at me. He said he saw his daughter-in-law using firewood stove for heating hot water for a bath. He said we can take it to Hyderabad and stack it up. I don't know how you will convince him."

She added, "Now it's you and Nanna, do whatever you want."

Kodandaramayya, smiled at her and said to her, "Don't worry. Nanna has his ideas, but he is never rigid. He will listen to logic. I will talk to him and explain." Sita said, "Of course, he will listen to you. You are his son," and smiled. Kodandaramayya, of course, could convince his father without much difficulty, saying, "Nanna, the amount of money we have to pay to transport, will be much more than the cost of the firewood if we buy it there. Sriramulu agreed immediately.

After lunch, Sriramulu went in and brought the money he got from selling the house and handed it to Kodanda to use the money appropriately. He said, "It will also cost some amount for this move." Kodandaramayya smiled and said, "I have money for the move. We don't have to touch any part of this money; instead, we will save it for Sita's marriage. From now on, don't worry about any financial matters; you have done enough. Just come and relax. Spend time with your grandchildren. They are excited and waiting for you back home."

Everyone let out a sigh of relief and got back to packing.

All the villagers started visiting them for one last time to say goodbye to Sriramulu and Subbamma. The whole village became emotional about the family moving away. Kodandaramayya, Sita, and their parents went to Chandrala to bid farewell to his aunt and cousins. Lakshamma was sad to see her brother's family leave. She said, "Annayya, since you and Subbamma moved here, I was confident that you are here with me. Even after my husband passed away, I was not shaken up. You have always been there for me. It will be a big void for me and my children once you leave. But I understand that you have no choice. You have to be with your son." After a big family lunch, they went back to Ganapavaram. Venkateshwarulu, Kodanda's cousin, accompanied them all the way to Ganapavaram. He helped in arranging trucks for moving. A taxi was arranged to take them to Hyderabad with a few valuables. The whole village came to bid goodbye.

Many of Subbamma's companions got emotional since she was a mentor, sister, and adviser for all of them. They would not stop talking to her. When it was getting late, Kodandaramayya had to finally intervene. With folded hands, he said, "Please let us go. I am taking my mother so she can spend time with her grandchildren, and I can take good care of both my parents in their old age. Please don't cry. I understand your love and affection for them. The way you are crying, it's like Rama and Sita are heading off to Aranyavasam." (Aranyavasam is when Rama and Sita went to the forest for 14 years from Ayodhya. All the citizens of Ayodhya were crying to bid farewell to Rama and Sita in the epic Ramayana)

He further said, "You can always come and visit them in Hyderabad whenever you want. Thank you all for everything. But now, it's time we get going."

He slowly helped his mother to get into the taxi, and his sister Sita followed him. Sriramulu waved his hand at everyone and got into the car. Kodandaramayya raised his hands in pranam, waved, and got into the car, then sat down with a heavy heart. With tears in their eyes, they bid farewell.

Kodandaramayya thought, "This is the one thing I always wished for. I wanted that my parents should live with me since they have had enough hardships. I want them to relax and live without a care in their lives."

Sriramulu, the brave man who never looks back when a decision is made, leaned back and closed his eyes for a second as though he is putting everything behind. For him, being with his son was what he ultimately wished for, and he literally felt that he had relinquished all his mundane responsibilities. On the other hand, Subbamma was filled with apprehension and uncertainty, she closed her eyes as though she had no energy to think further. Sita thought her commute between Hyderabad and Ganapavaram will finally come to an end. She hoped to find a job and stay in Hyderabad continuously to gain some work experience. She further thought 'the hunt for the groom will start seriously, and one more responsibility for my brother.' She did feel sad to leave Ganapavaram, where she was born and brought up.

They all reached Hyderabad late in the night. The children woke up and were excited to see their grandparents arrive. Satyavathi quickly arranged for their dinner and made sleeping arrangements for her in-laws. The truck arrived 3 days later with all their belongings from Ganapavaram. Subbamma took over the kitchen. She would cook the morning meal and continued the ritual of offering food to God every day after performing pooja as she used to do in Ganapavaram. It was not an easy ritual. Every day in the morning, she had to thoroughly clean the kitchen, after a bath, cook the food alone without anyone's help, and offer it to God after completing puja.

Until this time, Kodandaramayya and Satyavathi were only doing this on special festival days, but Sriramulu and Subbamma were used to this routine and wanted to continue. From then, this new ritual was established in the house. Whenever Subbamma was unable to do it, Satyavathi had to take care of it. Both Sriramulu and Subbamma would never eat before offering food to God. On the bright side, Satyavathi had time to take care of children and send them to school. She cooked dinner.

Sita, Kodandaramayya's sister, found a job in a primary school, where Kodandaramayya's younger daughter Sri Lakshmi and his two younger sons were studying.

One of his colleagues, Sri Krishnam Raju, who had a car, would come to the office in the morning in his car. After their office work, they all would go to the court in that car. Sri Krishnam Raju was from Godavari district, where he had a number of properties that he had to take care of, and he quit the practice in Hyderabad and moved to his village.

At this juncture, Kodandaramayya had no other choice but to buy a car. He bought a white second-hand Ambassador car, which he kept with him until he retired. In that car, he made several adventurous trips too.

The house always had visitors. It was not a big house. The two rooms in the front were used as his office. There was only one living room where they had to place all the household things, and a narrow veranda, a kitchen, and a dining hall.

The front office rooms were used for sleeping during the night. In this household, Kodandaramayya, his wife, 5 children, his parents, his sister Sita, and two of his nephews Satyavathi's brother's son, his sister's son all lived harmoniously. Sathyavathi's nephew, Kameswar Rao fondly remembers the affection he received from Kodandaramayya: "I spent more time living with mamayya (Uncle) and attayya (Aunt) than with my parents. Mamayya (refers to Kodandaramayya) was forthright, open, generous and the personification of love and affection, although a man of strong convictions and principles. I have been a recipient of his affection, love and generosity. What could I offer in return to him who had everything of real value, except a sastanga namasakaram (total prostration as a sign of reverence)."

In this small home they hosted several visitors and relatives who came from Ongole, Guntur, and Vijayawada. A couple of his distant cousins who were pleader clerks brought cases from the district court to the High Court and always stayed with them. They would stay for a couple of days to a week. Depending on their work. Apart from that, relatives coming to Hyderabad for medical reasons, some for official work, or some kind of training also stayed there. This could be anywhere from a couple of weeks to a month. There was no hesitation from both sides. They would come at any odd time, day or night, depending on the transport, even after the family had finished dinner and was ready to go to bed.

Satyavathi would heat up water for their bath, and by the time they were done, she would have the dinner ready. None of the family members ever felt any inconvenience with the sudden arrival of guests. Children would share beds to accommodate the guests. They never complained; in fact, they welcomed guests.

Kodandaramayya took immense care of his children. Once, when they moved houses, his son Raghu had to cross a busy road to go to his school. So, he personally trained his son how to look right and left, and then cross the road carefully among moving vehicles. He took him by the hand and crossed the road two or three times so that he could practice.

In spite of financial challenges, their children were always provided with basic needs. Kodandaramayya and Satyavathi made sure that they didn't miss out on essential things important for their holistic growth. He got them indoor and outdoor games, like carrom board, chess board, and a cricket bat for his son Raghu, who loved the sport. His daughter Parvathi wanted to learn the instrument Veena, and he readily joined her in Veena classes. He encouraged his children to read newspapers and biographies. As he did not have enough time to teach his children, he engaged tutors for them to improve their acumen in weak subjects.

Once the children grew up to a certain age, he made it a point that every Saturday morning, they all had to sit and recite chapters from the Bhagavad Gita. No matter what, they could never miss this. He also allotted a particular chapter to each of his children that they should learn and said that it would guide them in their lives. Most evenings, after his bath, he would read to his children and his wife from various religious books.

Certain days when he could spare more time, Kodandaramayya would walk to Sankara Mutt or attend spiritual lectures wherever they were taking place. Once in a while, he would walk to Tank Bund. He would often visit Sri Krishnadevaraya Hall where some literary talks were conducted. He also became a member and borrowed books from the library.

Distances never mattered to him. He always walked wherever possible. Sometimes he would take his older children along with him on these walks and tell them anecdotes from his life experiences. He would ask questions about general knowledge. He would also ask them about their day and encourage them to talk. On one of those walks, Parvathi, his eldest child, saw a big billboard of the movie Amrapali. She had just finished reading the story and said to her father, "Daddy, do you know the story of Amrapali that I just finished reading? Can I tell you?" He replied, "Please do, I really don't know."

By the time she finished her story, they reached the destination where they were going. The theatre, which was right in front of the place they went to, was screening the movie Amrapali. Kodandaramayya looked at it and asked his daughter, "Do you want to go and see the movie? Let me see how they have made the movie of your story." Of course, Parvathi was overwhelmed. Kodandaramayya asked her to go to the office in the theatre and inform the folks at home so they would not worry. When the movie was done and as they were coming out, Parvathi asked her father, "Daddy, how is the movie? Did you like it?" He looked at her, smiled, and said, "Actually, your story is better." Parvathi was ecstatic. Many a time he was spontaneous and quick with praise to encourage people.

Kodandaramayya met a Veda pandit, Kutumba Avadhani, who came to Hyderabad from Vijayawada. Kodandaramayya took to him instantly and learned Sandhyavandanam (Morning prayers) from him. Since then, he would regularly perform Sandhyavandanam both times, morning and evening. He helped Sri Kutumba Avadhani to settle down in Hyderabad. He thought, 'We need such Veda pandits in Hyderabad to teach people who are interested in scriptures and other knowledge of Sanatana Dharma.' He went to great lengths to make sure he remained in Hyderabad.

Avadhaani Garu wanted to go back to Vijayawada since he was unable to make ends meet. Kodandaramayya asked him what he would need in order to stay back in Hyderabad. Avadhani Garu said, "Whether I eat or not, I can remain if I have a house where the landlord will not ask me to vacate whenever he wants." Kodandaramayya said, "Leave it to me. I will take care of it.."

He then started collecting funds to build a simple house for Avadhani Garu. Eventually, with his efforts and Avadhani Garu's luck, Kodandaramayya made it happen. Avadhani Garu sold the house he had in Vijayawada, and with that money, he bought a small piece of land in Ashok Nagar. With the money Kodandaramayya had raised for him, he built a humble abode. He lived in Hyderabad for a long time and became a popular veda pandit. Many sought his advice on religious matters and spiritual knowledge.

Kodandaramayya's oldest daughter accompanied her father to the housewarming ceremony of Avadhani. She came back and asked her mother, "How come we don't have our own house, but father has helped Avadhani Garu to build his own house?"

Satyavathi said, "This is how your father is. When something is needed to be done, he just does it. Don't worry, his goodness will help us eventually."

Whenever the family moved houses, she asked her father, "How come we don't perform housewarming ceremonies?" Kodandaramayya would laugh loudly and say, "Oh, she wants to perform a housewarming ceremony for a rented house!" and patted her lovingly. When we build our own house, we can have a nice housewarming function. At that age, the daughter couldn't understand much, but she thought her parents were very special.

Kodandaramayya was busy with his growing law practice. At the same time, he was pursuing his spiritual life seriously. He kept reading Kavyas, Upanishads, mythologies, etc. He started going to the Shiva temple in Kachiguda and started performing Abhishekam (a ritual to pour water and milk on the Shivalinga as an offer of prayer) on every Maha Shivratri (a festival invoking Lord Siva). This practice he continued until the very end. Every Maha Shivratri, he would fast and perform Abhishekam at midnight, which is called lingodbhava kalam (the time when the Siva Linga first emerged on its own). The whole family participated. Later on, he would do abhishekam on every Masa Sivaratri. (Sivaratri which comes once a month) Even it fell on a weekday, he would go early in the morning to the temple, perform the abhishekam, come back, and then go to court. After a few years, the priest used to come home to perform the Abhishekam.

Learning Rudram (Vedic chantings on lord Siva) crossed his mind. But immediately, he became apprehensive, thinking, "Can I learn at this age?" One has to start learning any Vedic chants at a very early age as the voice has to be trained. It is like music. The vocal chords have to be trained early on. He asked Avadhani garu, "Will I be able to train my voice, which is no more tender and became rough with arguing at court?" Avadhani garu, with all his respect and affection for Kodandaramayya, took up the challenge, encouraged him saying, "Why not? If you have true desire, Eswara will help you. Let us look for an auspicious date and start." They did start. In the beginning, it was quite a challenging task. He could notice some frustration in Avadhani garu's face sometimes. Kodandaramayya would say, "I am unable to get this note, wonder if I ever can." Avadhani garu patiently persuaded and encouraged him by saying, "You will get it. Practice a few more times." So, it went on, and finally, Kodandaramayya did learn and performed Abhishekam himself, every day by chanting Rudram. Satyavathi and the older children felt the beautiful vibrations and a certain kind of energy around them. It was a family journey.

He took his parents to Srisailam, Bhadrachalam, Tirupathi, and Kalahasthi on a pilgrimage, performing a son's duty of taking the parents on pilgrimages.

The way Satyavathi and Kodandaramayya lived their lives was a lesson for their children. They never had to sit them down and give lectures. Satyavathi, in her own quiet way, showed her children to be patient, humble, and respectful. She taught her children to address their father as "Nanna garu" with respect. (Garu is equivalent to Ji in Hindi and Sir in English.) That one thing taught her children how to respect elders automatically. When someone addresses elders as "garu," they are automatically respected; one can't talk disrespectfully while addressing someone as "garu."

Satyavathi would say, "When you have four children, you cannot treat them all in the same manner. Though they are all your children, you need to know each one's likes, dislikes, and wants and raise them accordingly." True enough, when her daughter disliked eating food kept overnight, she was never forced to eat leftovers. Satyavathi would instead give it to her son who did not mind. Her mother-in-law, who observed this, reprimanded Satyavathi, saying, "What is wrong with you? Why are you giving overnight rice to the boy and hot rice to the girl?" Satyavathi said,

"It's okay, he does not mind so much, but this girl doesn't like leftover rice." This incredible parenting style of both Satyavathi and Kodandaramayya influenced the children and set an example by the way they lived their lives.

Kodandaramayya was a strict father and certainly a demanding husband. Whenever he was home, Satyavathi made sure that the children did not make noise and fight with each other. She always arranged things for him according to his convenience. She tried her best not to make him angry. He did have a streak of anger, which he inherited from his father. The children were afraid of him, but it was more respect than fear. All of them looked up to him. They always wanted to be in his good books and craved for his appreciation. Though he was busy with so many activities, he made it a point to spend some time with them every day.

Satyavathi served dinner for him and the children first, and then she would sit to eat at the end. At that time, all the children would sit around her to keep her company. Kodandaramayya would also be there, chatting with them about various topics. He would narrate things from his childhood, happenings in the court, stories from Ramayana and Mahabharata, or any other spiritual books. He would crack jokes, narrate short stories, and spend quality time with them. Then he would go and prepare for his cases for the next day. He never went to bed before 11 or 11:30 P.M. but woke up at 6 A.M. sharp or earlier, no matter what. He was slowly getting settled in his role as a senior advocate, building a reputation as a hardworking and a sincere advocate.

At the Supreme Court with Justice Venkatesam

Chapter 11
FULFILLING FAMILY OBLIGATIONS

Kodandaramayya had only two families related to them living in Hyderabad at that time. One was Dr. Vijayalakshmi's family, and the other was Subbayamma's brother-in-law. Though both families were not directly related, they became very close and visited each other whenever they could.

His cousin, Dr. Gurunatha Rao, used to come to Hyderabad once or twice a month to be with his wife, Dr. Vijayalakshmi. She couldn't join him in Vijayawada as she was posted in Hyderabad often. Whenever Dr. Gurunatha Rao came to Hyderabad, Kodandaramayya would have a bit of recreation. He would accompany Gurunatha Rao on some outings, or they would go and see a movie together. He only saw historical or mythological movies; he never went for social movies. Kodandaramayya was a friendly person but not a socialite.

His older sister, who was married, unfortunately, had things go weary. Her elder brother-in-law, who was managing the whole show, was unable to make ends meet, and the property was dwindling with no income coming in. He couldn't bear it and passed away, committing suicide. Kodandaramayya's brother-in-law was the youngest and a pampered child who was unable to do anything due to a lack of experience. As he was a Karanam (village head), he was getting some meagre amount, which was not enough to make ends meet. Kodandaramayya helped them whenever necessary. His brother-in-law fell ill and came to Hyderabad to see the doctor.

Kodandaramayya consulted the doctor and was advised that his brother-in-law should be admitted to Osmania Hospital for various types of tests. He was a heavy smoker too. He was there in the hospital for almost three months. During this time, his sister's entire family which consisted of her husband and her three children came to live with Kodandaramayya. This happened twice. Whenever his sister's family could not manage, Kodandaramayya helped them without a second thought.

His sister's only son came to live with them as there was no proper school in the village where they lived. He stayed with them until he graduated and found a job. One wonders about Kodandaramayya's strength and determination to follow dharma, and taking up responsibilities without finding it a burden.

How did he develop this kind of character? Perhaps he also did not know. He is one of those who is naturally that way, who don't realize their fine qualities.

One of his colleagues, Sri Adinarayana Raju, mentioned to his daughter, Parvathi, "Your father had taken up a Herculean task. A normal person cannot pull this off the way he did. He has divine blessings." Parvathi thought, if my father hears this, he would say, "What Herculean task? I am living my life the way I am supposed to live." That is the kind of humility he lived with.

The search for a groom for Sita became the first priority for Kodandaramayya and his parents. But somehow, a suitable alliance was not forthcoming, which made Subbamma anxious. Finally, an alliance came. The prospective groom was working at the Reserve Bank. He also had two younger sisters, and the responsibility of their marriage was on him.

Before fixing the match, Kodandaramayya talked to his sister. He said, "Sita, this boy has several responsibilities to fulfil. He has 5 sisters and one elder brother. It doesn't look like he has any support from the family. You have a difficult path to tread. I want you to understand everything and make a conscious decision. Amma is insisting on fixing the match. I would like you to tell me what you want. I want you to be happy. Whatever you decide, I will support that decision and will be there for you, but think carefully before you make any decision."

Sita thought, 'What is this love my brother has for us? Although I can wait, how long will I be a burden to my brother? He also has aging parents to care for. I better go with what is in my fate.' Thinking along these lines, she gave her consent.

Kodandaramayya prayed to Tirupati Venkateswara Swamy that he would perform the marriage in his presence if all goes well. When he informed the groom's family, they too agreed. The auspicious day for the marriage was fixed.

Kodandaramayya organized a bus that accommodated 50 passengers. Both the groom's and the bride's families started early the day before the marriage. When the bus departed, it started to drizzle, gradually intensifying into a heavy downpour as the journey progressed.

Near Nellore, a town midway to Tirupati, a few relatives joined them. Satyavathi's brother, who joined them with his daughter and wife, approached Kodandaramayya and said, "What is this? With what courage are you undertaking this feat? In this heavy rain, how do you plan on going up the hill? The marriage is in the morning; will we be able to reach and get ready for the muhurtham?" Kodandaramayya smiled and said, "Let us see."

The other passengers were also feeling a bit tense, but did not say anything as no one had any solution. Kodandaramayya didn't say a word; his courage was being tested.

It was raining heavily as they reached Tirupathi and approached the foothills of Tirumala. The road going uphill was closed, and the security guard said that they would not allow the bus as it was past the time to go up. Kodandaramayya said, "Tomorrow is the marriage, if we don't reach now, we will miss the muhurtham timing. By the time the road opens and we go up, it will be too late." He requested the guards, saying, "This is almost a matter of life and death. My parents are very old, with lots of effort, this marriage has been fixed. If this doesn't happen now, a great misfortune will fall upon us."

He used all kinds of methods to convince the guards to let them go. The guards were also family men, apart from performing their job as guards. Somehow, he could convince them, and finally, the guards agreed to allow a car with the key people to go up and start the marriage preparations. They refused to allow the bus. They said the bus could go up the next morning as soon as the gates open. He then organized a guest house for the rest of the family members on the bus to stay the night.

Kodanda hired a taxi to take the groom, bride, his parents, and the brother and sister-in-law of the groom, the purohit, and himself, and 2 suitcases with important things for the rituals. Subbamma asked, "How can we go without my daughter-in-law?" This irritated Kodandaramayya, "The marriage can be performed without your daughter-in-law. She will come later, don't worry. Now, hurry, let's go!"

As they were about to leave, Vijayalakshmi, Gurunatha Rao, and his elder brother Satyanarayana, along with a few other family members, arrived in a car. Satyanarayana came to Kodandaramayya and said, "What is this adventure! If we miss this muhurtham, we can look for another auspicious date. How can you take such a risk?"

Kodandaramayya thought to himself, 'If I miss this, who knows how things will work out? How long will we have to wait for a new date? All of us will have to go back, and the expenses and arrangements will all go in vain. What if the groom and his family, or Sita, change their minds? How do we know the future? How will we pull it off? How will my parents, who have been worrying for so long, handle this.' He didn't say a word but only smiled.

Gurunatha Rao looked at the situation and fully understood the predicament of Kodandaramayya. He quickly intervened and said to his brother, "Annayya, let it be. He will manage." He then turned toward Kodandaramayya and said, "Nayana, you go ahead and do what you have to do. I will take care of the situation here and come up when the gates open. Just go, your courage will protect you." Kodandaramayya thanked him, thinking, "how well he understands me!"

Thanking the guards, he prayed and headed up the hill and thanked the Lord in his heart and said, 'Swamy! You know the situation better than me. Please be with us and protect us. I'm taking this step as I have no choice. It is on you.' The guard said, "Let Lord Venkateshwara be with you and protect you. I'm not allowed to do this but here I am." He opened the gates and allowed the car to pass. The adventure started, and the people in the car were dazed, and nobody spoke. Maybe all were praying silently. They reached the guest house safely without a glitch through the downpour. With a sigh of relief, they thanked Lord Venkateshwara. Kodandaramayya showed the quarters for the groom and his family and said, "Now get some rest." The cooks, priests, and others said they never expected the marriage to happen. Kodandaramayya said, "I didn't know either, but He brought us here," turning toward the temple. "We are alright, and we are here now, so the marriage will go on as planned." Through all this, he never once showed any sign of distress and agitation. Sita told this to her niece Parvathi later. He said to his parents and his sister Sita, "All of you rest a bit, we have a long day tomorrow and have to wake up very early." Subbamma, with affection, taunted her son, "You will do whatever you think you should, rain or shine. Now you too get some rest." By the time the buses arrived next morning safely at the marriage hall, some of the rituals were completed. They all thought and agreed with Kodandaramayya that if they hadn't left the previous night, they would have missed the muhurtham. His courage helped protect him and the family.

None of this touched him; he kept on doing what needed to be done. They all had the darshan of Lord Venkateswara after the marriage. Kodandaramayya carried out his plan of taking the relatives for sightseeing around Tirumala. He never thought, 'What a stressful time it is; somehow, the marriage is done, we skip everything and go home'. The next morning, they visited Alamelumangapuram and then headed home and reached Hyderabad safely. He performed all the necessary rituals, and Sita went to her husband's home. Both the groom's party and the bride's family were happy and content that everything went well without any glitches.

Once, when Kodandaramayya went on a pilgrimage, his father fell ill a few days after he left. The doctor said it is better that Kodandaramayya comes back. The family was worried and panicked. 'How to contact him? He just called a day before, and it will be a couple of days before he calls again.' They informed Bhagiratha Rao, who is his junior and son of Sri Venkatesam, who was like a family member. He also tried to contact Kodandaramayya through his advocate colleagues in North India. Somehow, that didn't work. They were all waiting.

In those were the days there were no cell phones, no video calls, only letters and telegrams. They didn't have an address to send a telegram to Kodandaramayya as he was traveling. However, due to some kind of premonition, he suddenly felt like coming back. Maybe the love and affection of the father and son was drawing him to return. Sriramulu started saying, "Will I be there to see my son? I can't leave without seeing him. Why did he have to go on a pilgrimage when his aged father is here? What is the urgency? Is it important to take care of his father or to go on a pilgrimage?" Subbamma and the grandchildren tried to console him. The grandchildren said, "Grandfather, he's coming soon, don't worry, you won't go anywhere without seeing your son."

Kodandaramayya arrived soon enough. He sat on his father's bed, holding his hand, and said, "Nanna, I will never leave you and go anywhere. From now onwards, as long as you're there, I will not leave home. Now, don't worry, I am here, no more trips for me." Surprisingly, Sriramulu got better within a couple of days. Kodandaramayya never took another trip as long as his father was alive. Sriramulu got better in no time.

In a happy mood with his wife Satyavathi

Sister Venkayamma and her husband Narasimha Rao

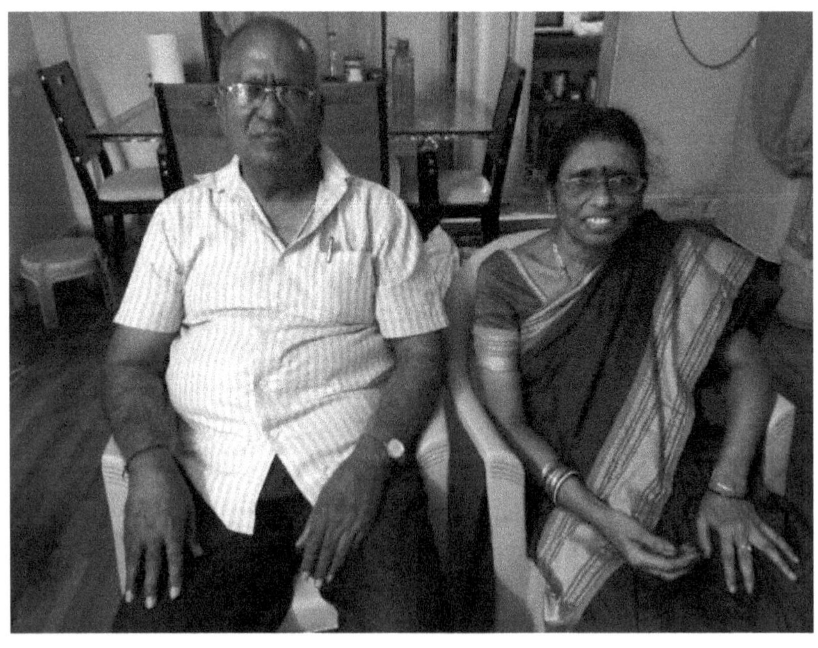

Sister Sita and her husband Hanumantha Rao

Chapter 12
LAST OF THE MUNDANE RESPONSIBILITIES

Both Satyavathis' and his parenting style were effortless, natural, loving, and affectionate. Satyavathi made sure that the children were never disobedient towards their father. On the other hand, she consoled and supported them when she felt their father was too harsh or strict with them. She would also explain to Kodandaramayya from time to time that he had been too strict, which may not be good for them.

Life had found its own rhythm. His parents were living with him, sisters got married, children were studying and growing well, and he was pursuing his spiritual path through various modes. He attended a course on Panini's Ashtadhyayi to familiarize himself with the roots of Sanskrit grammar. After he finished the course, he also enrolled his older daughter, Parvathi, and older son, Raghuram in the course.

Time passed, and one night, Sriramulu fell ill all of a sudden. He could not move his right hand and right leg. Dr. Vijayalakshmi diagnosed him with a paralytic stroke, and he had to be hospitalized at Osmania General Hospital for almost three months. Subbamma served him relentlessly. After coming home, the fighter Sriramulu would hold his right hand with his left hand and tried to write, as his right hand was incapacitated. He would drag his right leg and, with the help of a walking stick, tried walking. He himself would massage his leg several times with different oils, and finally, he walked with a limp. He was fed in the beginning, but he mastered eating his food himself with a spoon. Even the doctors wondered at his perseverance and independent nature.

Despite being busy with his professional and spiritual practices, Kodandaramayya never neglected his family or his social obligations. He would attend all family and friends' functions. His family, including extended family, had great respect, love, and affection for him. Anyone who came in contact with him respected him and wanted to develop long-term relationships. His children always sought his approval.

Kodandaramayya gave importance to dressing well. He used to say, "God gives us personality, and we have to enhance it by properly maintaining it and dressing well." He encouraged his children and appreciated them when they dressed well. When the children, especially the girls, got dressed up, they would go to him and ask, "Father, how do I look?" He would smile and say, "Yes, of course," and would never complete the sentence. Then he would laugh loudly and say, "Who are you? My children." He always wore only white clothes: a white shirt and white trousers. The only exceptions were sometimes off-white or a brown coat. At any given time, he never had more than five or six shirts. When any of his children or grandchildren complimented him by saying, "You are looking smart," he would laugh and say, "Wait, wait, let me shave and then you can see how I look," making everyone laugh. When he was in a jovial mood, his daughter Parvathi, once asked him "Daddy, when you were in college did you have any girls among your friends." Everyone became still, thinking what is wrong with her how could she ask such a question? She is in trouble. Kodandaramayya looked at her for a second, laughed loudly and said, "I did not have any girl friends but before my marriage I would look at girls sometimes, Once I got married never looked at any girl with a different thought." looking at his daughter, he said with a mocking smile, there did you get your answer and laughed. Everyone smiled and relaxed. That spoke volumes about him

Subbamma started saying to her son that he should start thinking of building a house and buying jewellery for her daughter-in-law. He would smile at his mother's desires for him and his family.

Life does not go without upheavals. Kodanda's second sister, Sita's husband, faced health issues. There was no one who could help from his family. She and her three children, along with her husband, came to Kodandaramayya's house. Of course, Kodandaramayya rose to the occasion. He took up the responsibilities of a father for his sister. His brother-in-law's job was in jeopardy, and Kodandaramayya had to talk to the manager to solve the problem and ensure he would not lose his job. His brother-in-law was hospitalized, given appropriate treatment, and recovered, continuing his job.

After a couple of years, this occurred again. With unwavering courage and always doing the right thing, both Kodandaramayya and Satyavathi took up the responsibility and successfully fulfilled the task a second time. He got his brother-in-law treated again, and again he got better. His sister's family came out of these hardships. All three of their children studied well and settled abroad.

When Parvathi, Kodandaramayya's older daughter, was in her second year B.A., Sriramamurthy, who was Kodandaramayya's mentor from Vijayawada, came to visit Kodandaramayya on some official work and saw Parvathi. He casually asked Kodandaramayya whether he was thinking of arranging a marriage for Parvathi. Kodandaramayya said, "I am not looking, but if there is a good proposal, why not?" They left the conversation there. Sriramamurthy later called Kodandaramayya and said that his cousin's son had completed his Ph.D., and they were looking to get him married. He highly recommended the family and the boy. Both the families, the boy and the girl met. Kodandaramayya, made his own inquiries about the boy and family, and was fully satisfied, agreed to the alliance. He invited all the senior advocates, judges, and other acquaintances. This was the first opportunity for him to interact and invite his colleagues in a social setup, which was much needed at that stage of his career. After Kodandaramayya performed his daughter's marriage, less than a couple of years later, Kodandaramayya and Satyavathi became young grandparents.

Around this time, Kodandaramayya met the famous shipping magnate Jayanti Dharmateja along with his daughter and his six-month-old granddaughter. Dharmateja saw him and said, "Oh, wow, here we see a handsome young grandfather." Kodandaramayya was thrilled at that comment. He said, "Yes, a proud one too." He used to repeat this many times to his family, saying that, "Dharmateja said that I am a young, handsome grandfather." He savoured certain moments and enjoyed these little pleasures.

His father had a second paralytic stroke and was hospitalized. This time he lost speech too. Doctors recommended taking him home and keeping him comfortable as there was not much they could do in the hospital. He was brought home, and within a few days, he passed away at the age of 84. Kodandaramayya was standing there holding his father's hand. Sriramulu could not speak, but looking at his son, he made a gesture that he is leaving. A man who lived with unshaken courage all his life left this world with the same courage, without a trace of fear in his face. It was an incredible experience for onlookers.

Losing his father was Kodandaramayya's first painful experience, and he missed his father dearly. For a long time, he would talk to his family about his father and shared numerous anecdotes about him with his children.

The landlord of the house he was living in would periodically ask Kodandaramayya to vacate. Though he had great respect for Kodandaramayya, he had his own intentions. He wanted to sell the house and was concerned about the difficulties of removing long-term tenants. Each time, Kodandaramayya would talk to him and convince him to extend the stay. This continued for a while. Eventually, the landlord sold the house to someone else, who rudely asked Kodandaramayya to vacate, threatening legal action. Kodandaramayya, amused, thought, "Oh, he wants to take legal action on a senior lawyer," but realized that it was time to move. After searching hard, they found a house in Venkateswara Colony in Narayanguda and relocated.

Kashi Vishwanath, his second son, along with a friend, wrote the entrance exam for NDA (National Defense Academy) and was selected. When he told Kodandaramayya about this, he didn't know what to say. This was a surprise. He thought about it, made a lot of inquiries, and he explained to Vishwanath that, "I have given a lot of thought to this. I think this is not suitable for us. Joining the army does not go along with the way of life we chose."

He said he's not worried about giving his son to the nation, but the lifestyle of an army person does not gel with the way they lead their lives. Kashi Vishwanath, of course, could not oppose his father. He joined in aeronautical engineering. It is interesting to note that the children obeyed their father fully, and he too, without being too rigid, gave them enough freedom. From both sides, there was flexibility, respect, and understanding.

One by one, the children finished their college education. After finishing his M.Sc., his oldest son, Raghuram, somehow did not want to go for further studies in the scientific field, he wanted to do law. This was another surprise, in a way, it was a pleasant surprise for Kodandaramayya. Raghuram joined Osmania University for a degree in Law. He later told his siblings that he wanted to be a lawyer, to be close to the parents, and take care of them.

Kodandaramayya's youngest son, Narasimha, joined B.A. in Nizam's College. His nephew, his oldest sister's son, Hanumantha Rao, joined B.Com. Sri Lakshmi, Kodandaramayya's second daughter, after completing B.Sc., somehow did not want to pursue further education in sciences. She joined Central University to do a masters in philosophy. Kodandaramayya was indeed very happy. Philosophy, of course, was his favourite subject. Lakshmi was an academic achiever, and Kodandaramayya was very proud of her.

When she was in her final year of MA, a colleague of Kodandaramayya visited him and saw Sri Lakshmi. He brought a proposal for her. His maternal uncle's son was doing a Ph.D. in the U.S. They were looking for a girl for him.

Both families, the boy, and the girl met. Horoscopes were matched. Anything Kodandaramayya did, he did with utmost care. He made his own inquiries about the boy and the family. After being fully satisfied, he agreed to the marriage. By now, Kodandaramayya's name was recommended for judgeship. He needed to perform the wedding in a manner where he could invite people from his profession. The wedding took place at Durgabai Deshmukh's B.Ed college in a grand manner. After the marriage, Lakshmi went to the U.S. along with her husband and returned to India after her husband successfully completed his Ph.D. Kodandaramayya was pleased that they came back without settling in a foreign country.

Both his daughters, who went abroad, came back and settled in India which made him very happy. He often used to tease his wife, saying, "How come you found sons-in-law, Bindu Madhav and Shankar, both having doctorates?" He used to tell his sons-in-law that they are not sons by law, but sons in fact. Both his sons-in-law had great respect and affection toward him.

Kodandaramayya wanted to perform his older son, Raghuram's 'Upanayanam' (thread ceremony). Raghuram was in his first year of MSc. Despite wanting to perform this ceremony sooner, circumstances hadn't allowed it. Family priorities always came first for him. His immediate family included his parents, siblings, and anyone who needed help, he had to address that first. Taking care of them was the first priority. He enjoyed celebrating happy occasions. This is his elder son's upanayanam, which is an important ritual to be performed. Excited and happy to perform the function, he was personally managing all the arrangements.

One day after completing shopping, and getting into the car, he suddenly fell unconscious. The driver held him and helped him into the car. He regained consciousness immediately, thought something is not right, and asked the driver to head to Dr. Vijayalakshmi's house. Dr. Vijayalakshmi and her brother, Dr. Shantharam, took utmost care and after conducting certain tests, he was diagnosed with a vascular attack, requiring complete rest. The family was in shock. Kodandaramayya had to postpone the ceremony,

Despite the setback, Kodandaramayya faced the challenge with a smile. Doctors advised him against climbing stairs for few days. As his his residence was on the second floor. He stayed at Dr. Vijayalakshmi's house for a week. He thought, "God, what is this test you are putting me through!" But he took the challenge with a smile.

During this time, he engaged himself in spiritual conversations with his guru, Jagannatha Sastry, who was a great devotee of Sri Krishna. Kodandaramayya asked him, "Sir, please ask your Lord Krishna, what is this play, what is he doing with me." His guru, full of affection toward Kodandaramayya, said, "I have already asked, and I got a message that you have to publish books and have much more to accomplish, and that nothing serious would happen to you." Surprised, Kodandaramayya said, "What books and what am I going to publish?" To that, he replied, saying, "I don't know anything; this is the message I got, and I am telling you. But I am sure you will be fine." With the prayers of well-wishers and the divine grace, Kodandaramayya recovered swiftly, returning to court within ten days. Six months later, he performed his son's Upanayanam in Tirupathi as planned.

80th Birthday celebrations

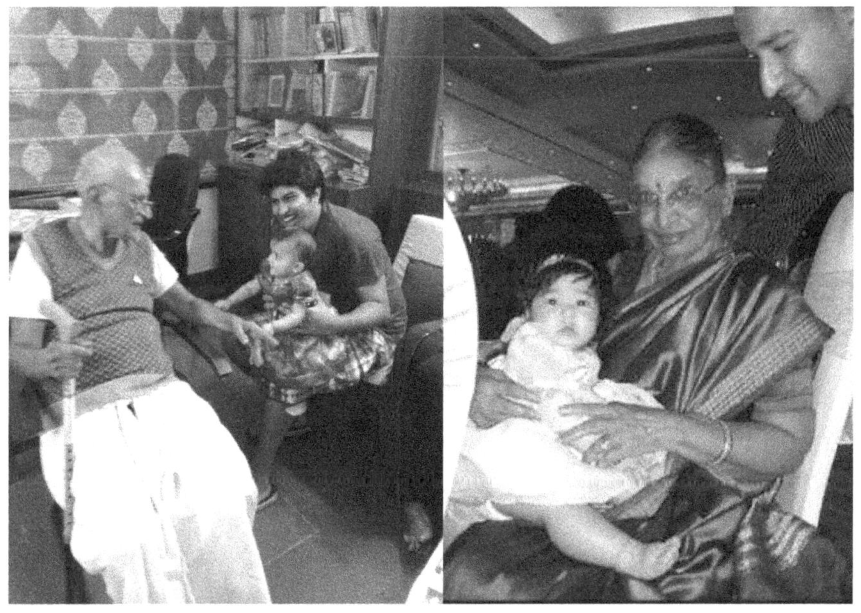

Enjoying with great grand children

Subbamma with eldest grand daughter, Parvathi

Chapter 13
TREADING THE SPIRITUAL PATH

Subsequent to starting his own practice, Kodandaramayya begain to steadily grow both professionally, financially, and spritually. The diligent sadhana he had been undertaking began to bear fruit, providing a deeper meaning to his life's pursuits. Dharma was his guiding principle, a philosophy that transcended words and found expression in his everyday actions.

By this time, Kodandaramayya had made a name for himself as a successful senior advocate. Kodandaramayya was busy with his growing law practice. At the same time, he was pursuing his spiritual life seriously and began practicing the three phases of Sravana, Manana, and Nidhidysana.

His colleague, Sri Krishnam Raju, said about him, "His quest for knowledge is unparalleled. He is kind, pious, and righteous."

Kodandaramayya's intense spiritual sadhana on his personal front continued without any interruption. Though he was busy with his career as a lawyer, he always made time for his family. Almost every other week, guests would come, but his routine never changed, except for slight adjustments in timing based on his office work. He allotted a lot of time to reading spiritual literature. He then plunged into reading Upanishads and started expanding his library.

He would always bathe both in the morning and evening to perform his Sandhya Vandanam, and then have his meal no matter how late or busy he was. Even on days when he slept at midnight or later, he always woke up at 5:30 A.M. in the morning. Regardless of his work demands and personal responsibilities, nothing would prevent him from his morning bath and prayers. His discipline was incredible. He never entertained thoughts like, "Oh, today is Sunday or summer vacation, I can skip something or wake up late."

Life was going in a rhythm; his mother was living with him, his sisters had got married, children were studying and growing well, and he was pursuing his spiritual paths through various modes.

Whenever Paramacharya of Kanchi Sankara math came to Hyderabad, he always had his darshan and never missed his talks. Satyavathi also would go when time permitted and she had a respite from housework. Kodandaramayya had developed immense devotion toward Kanchi Paramacharya, who became his spiritual guru. Around this time, he came in contact with Sri Ramamurthy Renu, who was very close to Paramacharya, and learned a lot about the guru through him.

A college mate of Kodandaramayya used to run down our epics and say, "These books Ramayana and Mahabharatha are like diseases in our society. Why Rama is considered a God? We have to annihilate all these so our society would be better. He is considered great because he was a devoted son! Why is that quality given such importance? Why do I need to give respect to my parents? They have not done anything special for me. It is because of their own enjoyment I was born."

These utterances pained Kodandaramayya very much. He thought, 'I have to read these epics thoroughly, so I understand what is there in them and get to the bottom of the truth.' He never argued without having authentic information. When in doubt, he would go to great lengths to get the correct information.

That is when Kodandaramayya started to look for a copy of Valmiki Ramayana with a word-to-word translation in Telugu. He could get the direct information without any author's bias and imagination. To his dismay, he could not find any such publication to his satisfaction. The seed of publishing such a Ramayana with word-to-word translation and commentary was sown in his mind, making Jagannatha Sastry's utterances come true.

With zeal to understand various religious thoughts, he thoroughly read the Quran, Bible, both old and new testaments. He was once invited to give a talk at an Islamic association. Addressing the audience, he said, "Brothers, have you all read the Quran thoroughly?" Only a few hands were raised. Kodandaramayya said, "I read it completely. Please read this scripture thoroughly. Once you do that, you will have peace and prosperity. No other religion teaches brotherhood as well as Islam. Once you have that brotherly feeling toward your fellow being, the world will be a beautiful place to live." Everyone appreciated it so much; he got a standing ovation. They said, "Sir, you must come again and talk to us."

Talking about Christianity, he used to say that "Compassion, service, and charity are the key components of that religion, while brotherhood is the highlight of Islam. If a person inculcates these qualities, there will not be any negativity in this world."

In his spiritual quest, Kodandaramayya began meeting and making acquaintances with Sanskrit and Telugu scholars at various literary and spiritual gatherings. A strong bond developed with some of these prominent individuals.

Sri Salaka Raghunatha Sarma, a great Sanskrit scholar, became very close to him. Kandada Ramanujam Chari, whom he used to fondly call Ramayanam Master garu, and Padma Sri Pullella Ramachandrudu, who is also recognized as Mahamahopadhya, a great Sanskrit and Telugu scholar, were associated closely with him.

He developed a close association with Veda pandits like Sri Dongre Sastry and a few others. It is important to mention Sri Lanka Sitarama Sastry, whom he knew from Guntur and who also moved to Hyderabad almost at the same time as Kodandaramayya. He was very knowledgeable and someone who followed the austerities strictly. Challa Venkateswarulu also moved to Hyderabad from Guntur; he was like a family purohit, performing all the pujas and weddings in the family.

His association with eminent Veda pandit Sri Vuppuluri Ganapathi Sastry, who was a Padma Bhushan awardee, and a great Sanskrit and Vedic scholar, writer, and a spiritual teacher, was significant. This association resulted in Kodandaramayya becoming the Chairman of Vuppuluri Ganapathi Sastry Veda Sastra Parishad, which was founded by Sri Sastry himself. It was a great honour. He accepted it humbly and worked relentlessly towards the cause of the Veda Parishad.

Around this time, Kodandaramayya felt settled professionally and also financially. Not that he had excess money, but he was able to manage his family life without much struggle. This is when he bought a 500 square yards land near Mahavir hospital in Chintal Basti area, the first property he ever owned.

He had incredible faith in divine intervention. Like any other parent, he too had certain wishes for his children. Something he noticed in his older daughter's horoscope was a bit worrisome for him. He prayed to God, quoting the shloka from "Mookam karoti vachalam, pangum langhayate girim." Meaning, 'you can make a dumb person speak and a cripple climb mountains. Can you not grant this small wish for me?' With intense faith, he initiated his daughter to Lalitha Sahasranamam and instructed her to chant every day without telling her the reason. He just said, "Chant this every day; it will give you all and protect you."

His wish was fully granted; he used to say, "I was blessed with more than I asked for." His younger daughter too was also initiated in Lalitha Sahasranama at the appropriate time. As she was completing her masters, Kodandaramayya was looking for a suitable boy. When it was getting delayed, he called his daughter and asked her, "Are you reading Lalitha Sahasranama regularly?" When he heard that she was not, he asked her, "Why not?" He then heard her saying, "You initiated my sister, she read it and got married right away, I don't want that, I want to study." Hearing that, he laughed aloud and said, "My dear baby, you are mistaken. Who said your education will not go on? Devi will give you whatever you ask for. Don't stop, continue chanting with devotion and your wish will be fulfilled."

He prayed in his own way and asked Devi, "Amma, you know who this girl's future husband is, and you must have already assigned him to her. Why do you trouble this poor man? Just show him the way." It may sound unbelievable, but it so happened: an alliance came, and her marriage was fixed. Lakshmi continued her studies even after marriage and got a Ph.D. This is a clear example of his faith and belief in the divine.

Kodandaramayya was proud and happy with the way his children have come up. He always cautioned them not to deviate from the Path of Dharma. He guided and advised even his older grandchildren. He said that it is the duty of elders to guide the children to tread the path of Dharma, whether they follow, or not, is their Karma. But we should do our duty and tell them.

He hardly reprimanded the children after they grew up, but, at the same time, always directed them to do the right thing. He never imposed his authority on his children or made them feel controlled by his ego. Instead, they sensed that his advice was given for their benefit, and thus, they felt compelled to follow it. If they didn't, they recognized it as their own lack of discipline or motivation, rather than feeling pressured by him. His approach was devoid of any desire to exert control or display authority, which was truly admirable. Even when he noticed his children not adhering to his guidance, he never reacted with anger or disappointment. Instead, he would simply encourage them to take action, smiling as he said, "What's the point of me telling you? Alright, let's start and do it now." This gentle yet firm approach instilled in them a sense of responsibility and motivation to comply.

When his eldest daughter was moving overseas, his advice was, "You are leaving the country, wherever you are, serve the humanity. Now you are a citizen of the world. Expand your horizons and serve." This advice helped her immensely. When she took up a profession as a counselor, she remembered her father's advice and worked without bias or discrimination and was greatly appreciated. Kodandaramayya had to move to a new residence allotted by the government, suitable for a High Court judge. At home, it was more or less the same. The only difference is that Satyavathi got sufficient assistance with household tasks, allowing her to finally find some rest and relaxation from her daily responsibilities."

At first, they found a big independent house in Shanti Nagar. After doing puja and planning to move, the landlord changed his mind and refused to let it out. Kodandaramayya was irritated and disappointed at the fickle-mindedness of people but never took any offense. He said, "Why are people so insensitive and inconsiderate about others?" Showing his endurance, not wasting his energy on trivial matters, he let it go. Later, he found a house in Durga Bai Deshmukh Colony and moved there.

Subbamma was so proud of her son and wondered how well he conducted his life and achieved all this. She thought it was all his hard work and sincerity. She made it a point to ward off Drishti (which is a warding off evil eye for her son) every evening when he returned from the court.

He had to shift his residence from Durgabai Deshmukh Colony to Srinagar Colony. While in Srinagar Colony, Kodandaramayya made it a weekly ritual to have tamarind rice prepared and distributed it to the poor people sitting outside the temple every Saturday evening for several years. This act of kindness became a consistent part of his life, reflecting his compassion for those in need.

The housing plot he bought near Mahavir Hospital in Chintal Basti, Hyderabad, was not the place where he would eventually build his house. He had to sell that plot and bought another in Jubilee Hills on road number 45. Things moved organically, and the house was built. He took great care and had the construction done with care. There were number of anecdotes about the care he would show the construction workers and the way he would ensure their well-being. He used to say that we can never repay them for the services they provide for us. Every day after coming back from court, he would visit the construction site and inquire about the workers' welfare. Periodically, he would take some food for them.

He named the house Sri Rama Sadanam, Abode of Sri Rama. In this house, countless Vedaparayanams were conducted. Every Maha Sivarathri Ekadasa Rudrabhishekam was conducted till lingodbhava kalam. Arsha Vignana Trust was formed, and he published the epics of Ramayana and Mahabharata. Two of his sons' marriages were performed. His grandchildren were born, and their marriages were also performed to the heart's content of both Kodandaramayya and Satyavathi. Satyavathi and Kodandaramayya became great-grandparents too in that house.

Kodandaramayya undertook many pilgrimages. He took his mother along on all the pilgrimages. Whenever the grandchildren asked Subbamma, "Grandmother, how does it feel to travel in an airplane?" The ever-adventurous Subbamma said, "Nothing different from a bus." They would all laugh.

Upon moving to his own house and fulfilling his mother Subbamma's wish, Satyavathi, his wife, indulged in her passion for gardening in the spacious plot, planting numerous plants to her heart's content.

One night after dinner, Subbamma went to her daughter-in-law and said, "I am having some discomfort in my back, apply some balm." Satyavathi applied a pain relief ointment. Later, when they were all going to bed, she told her daughter-in-law, "The medicine worked; I am feeling better. These people who invent all these things are quite smart." Satyavathi smiled and went to bed. After an hour or so, Subbamma walked into the main hall, saw one of the domestic helpers winding up the last chores for the night, and asked him to call her daughter-in-law as she is feeling uncomfortable. When he rushed upstairs to call Satyavathi, Subbamma reached for the bench and collapsed. Her second grandson, who was studying in the room close by, heard the noise, rushed to her, and held her, but by then she had collapsed. The pious and courageous Subbamma fulfilled her wish to leave this world without being bedridden.

A couple of years later, Kodandaramayya also lost his dear older sister, Venkayamma, whose son Hanumantha Rao had grown up in his home.

Raghuram, his eldest son, completed law and started practicing. Later, he became an eminent lawyer, a senior counsel, and is practicing in both Andhra Pradesh and Telangana High Courts, as well as in the Supreme Court. He was married to Savitri. They both, with their three children, Sri Ram, Patanjali and Vaishnavi lived with the father and mother and served them.

His son, Kasi Viswanath, is an aeronautical engineer turned entrepreneur who started his own software company. He was happy saying, "This boy is creating employment for a few people." Kasi Viswanath, his wife Arathi, and daughter Sidhi Kamakshi also lived with his parents and elder brother Raghu Ram in a joint family.

His youngest son, Narasimha, pursued a legal career in New Delhi. He was appointed as a Senior Counsel at the Supreme Court and eventually rose to become a Supreme Court judge in Delhi. He lived in New Delhi with his wife, Satya Prabha, son Bhrigu Aditya, and daughter Jyostna.

Hanumantha Rao, his elder sister's son, who lived with his uncle from childhood, graduated in commerce, found a job, got married, and took care of his parents.

All three daughters-in-law respected their in-laws and served them. He had 11 grandchildren and 12 great-grandchildren. Kodandaramayya found joy in seeing his family members thrive in their own pursuits.

Kodandaramayya remained humble and grounded, always emphasizing the importance of upholding dharma in one's actions. He guided and advised his children and the younger generation who sought his advice, encouraging them to follow the path of righteousness, while allowing them the freedom to make their own choices.

After the daily prayers

Garlanding Pamidighantam Venkataramanadas at Amba
Sathram, Bhadrachalam

Participating in cultural and spiritual activity

Pursuing literary and spiritual activity

Chapter 14
THE JUDGE

Kodandaramayya was recommended for the judgeship. But he was initially hesitant to take up judgeship. Sri Shivshankar, the Law Minister who knew Kodandaramayya personally, encouraged him to accept the position. Recalling his father's words about his horoscope indicating that he would have the power to authenticate official documents, Kodandaramayya smiled to himself, thinking of his father's love and faith, which had brought him to this stage. With humility, he accepted the offer. He ruminated, thinking, "What is the point of getting any laurels and ivy's when my father is not here to see?"

Interestingly, the night before Kodandaramayya was to be sworn in as a judge, he dreamed of his father who approached him, touched his head, kissed him, and then vanished. He became the sole individual from both his father's and mother's sides of the family to reach such heights. While many attributed his success to his discipline, unwavering commitment to goodness, courage, humility, and intense faith in God, Kodandaramayya himself did not entertain such thoughts but accepted everything as it came.

During his tenure as a judge from 26.7.82 to 30.8.88, Kodandaramayya authored a substantial number of judgments, with approximately 150 being full-fledged, reportable cases. These judgments not only showcased his expertise in land tenure and civil matters but also extended to administrative and constitutional law. Lawyers and judges alike praised the wide range of topics he addressed in his decisions. His judgments on the subject of contract law are considered to be decisions made with great expertise and precision.

Kodandaramayya was particularly noted for taking up and resolving a large number of civil cases involving complex issues, a task many judges before him had avoided due to the complications and time involved. However, Kodandaramayya took up those cases and disposed them with great expertise and ease. His dedication and competence in resolving such cases earned him great admiration and contributed significantly to the functioning of the court as an institution. Deciding important and popular cases brings name and fame to an individual judge. The most difficult part is to decipher complicated cases that demand great effort and application of mind to adjudicate and decide them. For this, only the individual judge's conviction and commitment to the situation matters. In fact, it is nothing but sacrifice as it is a totally selfless effort. He put his heart and soul into deciding all cases. There are many more decisions made by him that are reported judgments, which resolved disputes and provided a solution in the absence of a laid-down law. These decisions go unnoticed but have a direct contribution to the working of the system. A large number of pendencies are removed from the list of old cases pending in the court.

After his retirement, he was offered an assignment to head a special tribunal for the prevention of land-grabbing cases. He was not the first judge to have occupied the position of Chairman of this tribunal. It is well recognized that difficult and sensitive cases involving certain political heavyweights were not taken up for a long time. When he took over as Chairman, several sensitive cases, which had accumulated over a period of time, were in the long list of pendencies. Apart from that, lands involved in these matters were very valuable and situated in areas where property prices had increased multi-fold. It is said that immediately after taking over as Chairman, he took stock of the pending matters and directed that all these cases be listed for disposal. Many senior advocates appeared before him and asserted that these are sensitive cases and that they will take some time.

In no time, the advocates for the state and the private parties realized that this is a judge who means business and that they had no alternative except to prepare well and appear, and there would be no two ways about it. In fact, all the cases were taken up and decided by Justice Kodandaramayya. His judgments were later upheld by the Supreme Court.

There is another important aspect about his performance in this tribunal. For a long time, there was no record demarcating the lands with precision. This contributed to the pendency of cases where there were multiple claims on the basis of Inams and Grants, etc. As Chairman of the tribunal, he consigned various maps, information, data, and reconciled them with the correct existing topography of revenue survey numbers and identified their correct locations. His decision is now the blueprint and a benchmark for the resolution of many pending cases involving the identification of correct boundaries. His expertise in civil law, particularly the land and tenancy laws enabled him to dispose of a large number of cases to the satisfaction of the state and the contesting parties. His decision-making was based on a deep conviction in the rule of law combined with an appreciation of lived experience and a sensitive understanding of human vulnerabilities. Thus, he could do complete justice with equity, as observed by his younger son Justice P.S. Narasimha.

As he navigated his responsibilities as a judge, Kodandaramayya never lost sight of his duty to serve the people and uphold justice. His legacy lives on, not only through his reported judgments, but also through the countless cases he resolved, often going unnoticed, yet contributing to the functioning of the legal system.

During his tenure as a judge, Sri N.T. Rama Rao took oath as the chief minister for the second time. All the judges were invited to attend the ceremony. When Kodandaramayya went to the ceremony, he handed over a small note to N.T. Rama Rao. In the note, he wrote, "Rajyante Narakam Dhruvam," which means, "For a ruler, hell is inevitable." This implies that when one becomes a ruler, one will inevitably make mistakes in judgment and punish the innocent. Therefore, one has to face the punishment for these mistakes. The knowledgeable and open-minded person that he was, N.T. Rama Rao, looked at the note immediately, smiled, and nodded at Kodandaramayya.

Despite his professional achievements, Kodandaramayya's personal life remained largely unchanged. He maintained his daily routines and rituals, demonstrating the same level of dedication and attention to detail in his work as he did before he became a judge. He continued to uphold the values of integrity and fairness, leaving a lasting impact on those around him.

Throughout his career, Kodandaramayya worked alongside eminent judges such as Justice Jagannadha Rao, Justice Choudary, Justice Jeevan Reddy, and Justice Jayachandra Reddy, leaving an indelible mark on the legal profession through his dedication and commitment to justice. He worked with intense sincerity and dedication.

One evening, a certain gentleman known to Kodandaramayya for a long time came to meet him at home. His case had been allotted to Justice Kodandaramayya, and the final verdict was to be delivered the next day. Late in the evening, the day before the judgement was to be delivered, the attendant came to Kodandaramayya and said that the person involved in the case came to meet him. Kodandaramayya was surprised and said,

"How come he has come to meet me? Tomorrow is the final judgment to be given for his case, and why did he come to meet me now? Please inform him that I cannot see him and that he should leave." The man left disappointed and confused. The next day, Kodandaramayya announced in court that the judgment cannot be passed and explained what had happened, stating that the case should be transferred to another judge. The reason is that the judgment was given in favour of that gentleman. Kodandaramayya did not want anyone to mistake that the judgment was given in his favour because he visited him. This would have been perceived as a scandal, which was averted by his presence of mind, ensuring fairness and transparency in the legal proceedings (as recounted by his younger son justice P.S. Narasimha).

Satyavathi's nephew, N. Chandradhar, who practiced as an advocate, mentioned that Kodandaramayya gained the reputation that he used to be thorough on all aspects of Law. In particular, he was considered an expert in Civil, Revenue, and Land Laws. While rendering judgments, he used to conduct his own research about case laws relevant to the issues involved in the case, apart from the citations submitted by counsels from either side. He always attempted to make a mark for himself as a judge, and many of his judgments were reported. He was a pious man of integrity and had no preconceived notions or prejudices toward any of the members of the bar. He used to command respect from both the Bar and the Bench.

At the innaguration of a Magistrate Office

Relaxing at the Airport

Being honoured after retirement

Chapter 15
KARMA YOGI

From the time Kodandaramayya started his literary pursuits, he never took interest in any social or fictional literature. He often said, "Why do we need to read these social novels? Is life's drama not enough?" He felt that by reading such books, one's emotions come into play, and one moves away from reality and gets addicted to this without being able to come out of it. We get drowned in the unreal and lose sight of the real purpose of life.

He started off with reading biographies of eminent people. All the literature he selected somehow led toward a spiritual destination. He read kavyas along with Ramayana and Mahabharatha. Even in the philanthropic activities he took up, he searched for spiritual meaning consciously or unconsciously. But in his pursuit to find the truth, he would get frustrated and tired and would say, "How do we find the truth? Everything is confusing, and not even a glimpse of what is beyond is being experienced." But again, he would gather his energy together and continue his sadhana.

He once went to pay his respects to Paramacharya, but at that time Paramacharya was in mounam (observing silence). He signalled to Kodandaramayya, showing in action, "What do you want?" Kodandaramayya, with reverence, said, "Swamy, make me a Yauvannaswam" (which means a strong young horse). To that, Paramacharya again asked through action, "What will you do?" Kodandaramayya said, "Swamy, you can sit and ride on me." Swamy loudly laughed. Ramamurthy Renu, and the others present were so thrilled and touched. They said, "You made Swamy laugh wholeheartedly. You are blessed." A horse rider directs and leads the horse in the right path and takes him to his destination. Kodandaramayya hoped that the Paramacharya would lead him into the right path to his spiritual destination – such was his incredible faith in his guru and the divine.

His association with Sri Acharya Pullela Ramachandrudu led to discussions on translating the Valmiki Ramayana with word-to-word meaning, with complete meaning of each sloka along with commentary. He then requested Sri Pullela Raamachandrudu garu to take up the task, to which he happily agreed. Thus, the blessing of Sri Krishna, through Jagannatha Sastry, materialized. Arsha Vigyana Trust was born in 1983. A number of books, including all the Kandas of Ramayana, came to light.

Then he took upon himself the marathon task of getting the translation of all the 18 parvas of Vyasa Bharatha. This was done by Sri Salaka Raghunatha Sarma and Sri Kandada Ramanujachari. Kodandaramayya himself wrote introductions to these epics. Apart from this, he also wrote magnificent introductions to all Parvas of Mahabharatha in Telugu, bringing in concisely the salient features of all 18 Parvas.

After publishing the Ramayana and reading and understanding it thoroughly, he was prompted to take up the work of writing about the Ramayana. After toying with the idea, he went to Paramacharya to seek his guidance. Paramacharya heard his wish and said, "Many people wrote the story of Ramayana. You don't need to write the same." He then said, "Who is Purushottama (one who has great qualities, and one who is the best of men)?" Kodandaramayya said, "Who else but Sri Rama Ramachandra." Paramacharya smiled and said, "Then write about him. Write about Sri Rama, his qualities." Kodandaramayya caught the idea and wrote his first book, "Light of Ramayana," which was greatly appreciated by many.

In the introduction of his book Light of Ramayana, he said, "The theme of the book is to draw attention of the modern young men, emphasizing the fact that the several dharmas practiced by Sri Rama, the hero of the epic, are in the nature of faculties. The work illustrated the qualities of Sri Rama. Every human being should imbibe and practice these qualities to make his life successful and purposeful," he further says. "Dharma is not a mere religious precept necessary for spiritual pursuit alone. It is necessary for securing prosperity in one's own life."

Kanchi Paramacharya's message on the book says, "His holiness is pleased to note that Justice Kodandaramayya has written this book "The Light of Ramayana" bringing out in various chapters how Sri Rama practiced several facets of dharma, which are the life skills that should be followed by the younger generations." He listed the virtues of Sri Rama in his book. A few of them are: worship elders, show no jealousy, compassionate, never interested in quarrel prone conversation, not losing temper even if he is slandered, never utters a lie, and is courageous.

When one closely observes Kodandaramayya's life, one can sense that he has imbibed all these qualities. If not, he could not have conducted his life the way he did.

It is important to mention his special devotion to those whom he prayed and sought guidance for all his scholarly pursuits: Bhagavan Vedavyasa, Sri Gurudeva Datta, Maharshi Bhrigu, Sri Narada para Brahma and Sri Chandrasekhara Saraswathi Mahaswamy who was his paramaguru, Kurthalam Swamy, Mudikonda Venkatarama Sastry, Sri Tadepalli Raghava Narayana Garu, Advitanan Valluri Venkatesarulu, Viswanatha Satyanarayana Garu, Divakarla Venkata Avadhani Garu, Raghava Narayana Garu, R Somanchi Sri Ramulu Garu, and Devala Madhya

Sikhamani Garu are some of the great scholars and Veda Pandits he looked up to with great reverence.

Apart from publishing all the Seven Kandas of Ramayana and all the Parvas of Mahabharata, through Arsha Vignana Trust, he also brought to light two volumes of Brahma Sutra Bhashayas, Bhagavad Gita, Patanjali Yoga Darsanam, Sri Siva Panchastavi, Dasamaskhandam of Bhagavatham, and a few others.

He said that the epics Ramayana and Mahabharata were the two eyes of society. As such, he took up the work of writing on the Mahabharatha. Again, he planned to capture the gist of the epic, 'Message of Mahabharata,' which was published by Bharatiya Vidhya Bhavan. It is important to acknowledge that Sri Seshagiri Rao patiently typed all his writings.

For this monumental work, he wrote an introduction of 73 pages, giving the essence of Mahabharatha. He covered the topics in the epic, the facets of Dharma and Adharma, lessons from the epic stories, Punya and Papa, Sages, Apsaras, Mountains, Rivers, Kingdoms, and warriors, Darshana's and Vidya, Spirituality, religion, and many more topics relevant to study and learn for the present day. He said that, "The Epic Mahabharata is a Magnum Opus and multi-dimensional." Additionally, his contributions to publications such as Bhavan's Journal and Vedamatharam reflected his commitment to sharing knowledge and promoting Sanatana Dharma.

In his book "Message of Mahabharatha," he concentrated on the concept of Dharma, which is the message of the epic. He further added that he took up this task upon himself in the fond hope that reading of this book will promote understanding and cordiality among different religious and different communities of this country. With this view, he dedicated this "Magnum Opus" to the nation. In short, his message was that every citizen should imbibe dharma and act accordingly for the benefit of humanity.

The Vedic religion, now called the Hindu religion, enunciates non-dualistic philosophy. A true Hindu never accepts a Hindu Raj, apart from the mandate of our constitution for a secular state."

A few key points he summed up from the introduction of this book are essential to understand his anguish for the welfare of the country and the citizens. He noted that, "Each citizen must assimilate the spirit of others belonging to different communities and preserve their individuality and grow together." He constantly emphasized that citizens should not only fight for their rights, but also take up some responsibility, and a certain amount of sacrifice is needed in order for the welfare of the society and country. He was involved in the upkeep of many temples and donated funds to various holy places. Bhadrachalam, Simhachalam, Yadagiri, Srisailam, Gurukulam of Veda Bhavan, and the Durga temple in Vijayawada are a few examples.

He extended financial aid to Law and Sanskrit students, donated to the advocates' association, and gave financial aid to the poor patients in the hospital. He fasted on the death anniversary of Mahatma Gandhi to show his reverence for the father of the Nation. He continued to do this almost toward the end of his life. He used to say, "We have to learn from Gandhiji about the nature of sacrifice for society's well-being."

Addressing a gathering on one occasion, referring to the legal profession, he said that, "it had lost its appeal to the general public." He talked about the significance of professional ethics, saying that "we must practice law such that we can say, yes, I want my children and grandchildren to become lawyers." One must be proud of his or her profession and serve with integrity. By giving repute to your profession, you can acquire great respect. He further said, "For the money we earn, we must be willing to shed some blood." He was indeed a great personality committed to his profession.

A couple of sayings from eminent people mentioned in the introductions to his two books are worth noting here. They give us a deeper glimpse into what moved him intellectually and spiritually. He tried his best to follow these principles in his life.

The saint poet Rabindranath Tagore, "*We could never do justice from a mere sense of duty to those for whom one lacks respect. So, each religion should be respected, as each religion has its own spiritual heights. One in truth, and another in compassion, love, and yet another in equality. Hence, we should never try to destroy but to fulfil.*"

Veda Vyasa, at the end of the epic, said, "*Everyone should practice dharma and should not forsake it either for pleasure, for fear, for cupidity, or even for life.*"

His philanthropic works did not stem from an abundance of money. He minimized his personal needs. The second-hand Ambassador car he bought when he was a lawyer was what he used until he retired as a judge. He never bought another car after that. He never bought jewels for his wife or his daughters, nor did he invest money. Whenever he had a bit of extra money, his only thought was how to use it for the benefit of others.

He regularly performed Sri Rama Kalyanam at the Rama temple in Whitefield, Gachibowli. This temple was built under the guidance of Kanchi Paramacharya. Sri Rama Rao, a good friend of Kodandaramayya, built the temple of Sri Rama as per the instructions of Kanchi Paramacharya. Kodandaramayya was in close contact with the temple. He regularly visited the temple and attended Sri Rama Kalyanam on Punarvasu, the birth star of Sri Rama. Whenever he visited the temple, he made a point to give money to the cleaners, the musicians, and every other worker, apart from donations to the temple. He did this in every temple he visited. Taking care of the workers was very important to him.

He acknowledged his mistakes instantly; when he realized that he hurt someone, he would say, "Because of me, this mistake has happened. '*Chempalu vesukovali.*' I have to slap myself and correct it, and never repeat it again."

He made it a point to meet eminent people whenever he had a chance, not to ask for any favor but to show his respect to them. He sought inspiration from different quarters and often made it a point to meet people from different fields, be they literary scholars, statesmen, or even eminent people doing social work. There was always a desire to meet and pay his respects to them. When he visited Bombay after his retirement, he made it a point to meet the erstwhile PM of India, Late Shri Morarji Desai, and former President of India, Late Shri Shankar Dayal Sharma. He would meet them to get inspiration from these great personalities. Often these meetings were brief and to the point. He also met Late Shri Ramakrishna, President of Bharatiya Vidya Bhavan. He was greatly moved by the anecdotes narrated by Sri Ramakrishna about Shri K.K Munshi and his vision. Kodandaramayya would often beautifully narrate his experiences to his children with such enthusiasm and joy, almost childlike, that his children grew upon his experiences in their own lives.

Indeed, he managed his journey of worldly life and his spiritual pursuit so well that each mirrored the values of the other. He liberally applied his spiritual insights to his legal and judicial work. Conversely, his experiences as a lawyer and as a judge are reflected in his books on Light of Ramayana and Message of Mahabharata. There was oneness in all his activities as he excelled at harmonizing his professional, religious, social, and spiritual facets. It took a great deal of sadhana, against all odds, to attain such a balance, which became an intrinsic part of his being.

What stood him in good stead was his remarkable clarity about his values and priorities, coupled with an indomitable spirit. He lived life with a deep sense of his mission such that he never seemed to have any doubt or regret. Even in the most trying circumstances, his children never found him sad or depressed. He had clearly transcended all such emotions. He was truly Adeenaatma (beyond a feeling of self-pity), a quality of Sri Rama, that he extolled time and again, without perhaps realizing that he had himself evolved to that state.

His commitment to spiritual practices was unwavering. Apart from reading Ramayana, he practiced Ramayana Parayanam (reading with a certain rhythm and within a certain time and a certain number of times). He would start on Punarvasu (the name of the star when Sri Rama was born) and complete it by the next Punarvasu. Unless one does this with great zeal and dedication, it is a very difficult task. Despite the monumental challenge posed by this task, Kodandaramayya approached it with determination, embodying the qualities of perseverance and discipline. He did this parayanam more than 30 times. It is a marathon-like task. Even for the greatest of scholars, it is not an easy job. It is possible only for someone who is relentlessly seeking the truth.

He once confessed to Salaka Raghunath Sarma, "None of you know that the Mahabharata, which has one lakh 25 thousand shlokas, I read it three times." To this, Sarma said, "This is our duty. As Sanskrit scholars, we have to do this, but to my knowledge, no one has done this." He was astonished at the incredible dedication toward the spiritual quest of Kodandaramayya.

Whoever met him, he made them feel that they were important to him. He genuinely cared for them, always inquired about them and their families' welfare. He unconditionally extended his care and love.

He often emphasized the importance of preparing not just financially, but mentally, for retirement and old age. Just as one plans for a secure future with pension and life insurance policies, it's equally vital to cultivate spiritual practices to engage the mind in old age. Otherwise, one may find themselves at a loss on how to fill their time. He believed this preparation should begin early, ideally around the age of forty. He would only get frustrated or irritated when simple things were not done on time, or people around him were dishonest for trivial things.

When he was 73 years old, his hearing reduced. Eventually, he had to use a hearing aid, which was not very comfortable. At that point, he decided not to take up any official assignments, as his work required clear hearing. He used to joke when he started wearing the hearing aid, "Just wait, let me adorn myself with this jewel before I speak or hear."

It is common for the elderly to slip and fall, mostly in bathrooms. Kodandaramayya also could not escape this ordeal. At the age of 85, he fell and fractured his hip. But with his determination, through physiotherapy and other alternative treatments, he got up and walked back to normal. An unfortunate thing occurred at this time; he had to have a catheter to pass urine, which he could not get rid of, though he tried his best until the end. A urine bag was taped to his leg. With a lot of discomfort and pain, he pursued his spiritual and academic sadhana with unbeaten spirit. Whatever work he took upon himself, he would always do it effortlessly. He said that when we do our duty with concentration and responsibility, it can be done effortlessly. This is also a quality of Sri Rama, which he imbibed.

His routine never changed, except for a few modifications to his timings. He followed a strict diet, gave up eating sweets, and never went out except to attend important meetings when he was insisted upon by people who wanted him to be there. After the third edition of Ramayana and the second edition of Mahabharatha, he stopped active public participation. He continued his spiritual sadhana, reading various spiritual books in such depth that one felt he was preparing to write exams. He still read the newspapers regularly to know what was happening in the country and the world at large and would discuss everything with his children. His anxiety for the welfare of the country never stopped.

Around this time, he used to say, "Now the time has come to prepare for the journey." When some of his children asked for instructions, he would say, "I have nothing more to tell you. I have already said all I needed to. Now it is up to you." Practicing detachment, toward the end, he never gave any instructions or expressed any wishes. He never engaged in futile talk; he just did his personal sadhana.

In the year 2018, April, he was a bit unwell, nothing in particular, looked tired and a bit low in energy. In the month of May, it was the time for his mother's annual ceremony. Kodandaramayya performed both his father's and mother's annual ceremonies with incredible dedication and care every year. That year, because of his health, somehow, he missed the date. His sister Sita was always invited for the ritual. That year, when she did not hear from her brother about the annual ceremony, she called her brother and said, "Annayya, tomorrow is amma's ceremony. How come I didn't hear from you?" Kodandaramayya was shocked and taken aback and poured his appreciation and love on his sister, saying, "Amma, you have saved my day. How come I missed the date? What kind of mistake have I committed? Please come tomorrow with your husband, and now let me go and make preparations."

It was a very big deal for him. He was 92 years old, not too well, but still performed the ritual in a full-fledged manner.

After that day, his health started deteriorating. He was forgetting and started talking a bit deliriously. His sons, Raghuram and Kasi Viswanath, took him to Apollo hospital, and the blood test showed that his sodium levels were low, and that he should be admitted to the hospital. He and the family were reluctant but had no choice but to admit him as per the doctor's advice. He was treated with great care at the hospital as Sri Pratap Reddy, the founder of the hospital, knew him personally and had great respect for him. He never came back home.

On June 15, with all his children, grandchildren, and near and dear chanting Vishnu Sahasranama loudly, he left this world.

When he passed away, people came from various corners of Andhra Pradesh to pay their respects. Many said that because of him, they were able to have two-square meals. He helped people with their children's marriages, education, and employment. Even his children were not aware of the kind of charity he practiced. He lived by the adage that "what the right hand does, the left hand should not know."

Justice Sudarshan Reddy, in his message when Kodandaramayya passed away, said that "he did not save any material positions for himself, but the inheritance he gave his progeny was the example of his righteous conduct."

Every newspaper in Andhra Pradesh covered the news of his demise. All the senior advocates and Judges, including the Chief Justice, visited and paid respects. At the High Court, they held a condolence meeting and invited the family members. The courtroom was filled with people who knew him well - from advocates to judges, from registrars to administrative staff; all attended the meeting to pay respects to him. After the event, the court announced a holiday. All this is, in fact, was a great honour for a judge who was on the bench for only a period of 6 years and who passed away 30 years after his retirement as a judge.

Overall, Kodandaramayya's life can be characterized by a relentless pursuit of knowledge, a deep respect for tradition, and a genuine desire to serve others. His interactions with eminent personalities and his scholarly endeavours exemplified his commitment to personal growth and the dissemination of wisdom.

He strongly advocated for living a life free from mental and emotional stress. Setting an example for his children, he lived his life in such a manner. Even in the face of the most challenging crises, he remained composed and undisturbed, never displaying signs of distress or agitation.

Throughout his life, Kodandaramayya exemplified the values of integrity, compassion, and selflessness. His legacy continues to inspire future generations to uphold dharma and strive for the greater good of humanity. He left this world, practicing detachment and seeking liberation. He was regarded as a person who is courageous, upright, pious, and righteous by all those who knew him. He lived his life to the fullest.

An ideal way of living and concluding one's life - he stands as an example.

"Anayasa maranam, Vina dainyena jeevanam"

Dehante tava sayujyam, dehi me Kripaya Shambho
Dehime Parameshwaram

"An easy death, A life without anguish."

Toward the end, , kindly absorb me into you, Siva."

Karma Yogi

His House:
He built a humble ground floor, his sons built first and
second floors

REMINISCENCES

JUSTICE B.P. JEEVAN REDDY

Former Judge,
Supreme Court of India

Former Chairman,
Law Commission of India

Plot No. 202, Vamsirams Jyoti
Valencia

Road No. 2, Banjara Hills

Near Sagar Society Signal
Hyderabad - 500034, Telangana
Mobile : 98492 80544
justicebpjeevanreddy@gmail.com

MESSAGE

Justice P. Kodandaramaiah garu was known for his deep learning in law both as an Advocate and as a Judge. Civil and Constitutional laws were the fields of his expertise. The law reports of High Court of Andhra Pradesh speak of his masterly analysis of difficult legal propositions with great ease and felicity. His contribution to the development of law is memorable.

Justice P. Kodandaramaiah garu and myself sat together in a Bench for quite some time which gave me a unique opportunity to appreciate and admire his devotion to law, his judicial restraint (a quality much to be admired in a Judge) and clarity of thought. The moment he sat in the chair, he would write SRI RAMA on the paper before him and then commence his judicial work. He idealized Bhagavan Sri Rama. Justice P. Kodandaramaiah's strength of character and his approach to life was guided by the life of Sri Rama. His was a disciplined life. This was one facet of his life. The other facet is his religiosity and his enormous contribution to the promotion of ancient wisdom of India. He authored two learned treaties "Light of Ramayana" and "Message of Mahabharata' He founded Arsha Vignana Trust for promotion and propagation of our heritage. Through the instrumentality of this Trust, he got published several books including Valmiki Ramayana with all its kandas translated from Sanskrit to Telugu and explaining the meaning of each sloka. In similar vein, he got published all the parvas of Mahabharata as well, Two volumes of Brahma Sutras (together with their meaning) were also published through this Trust. For the purpose of translating Sanskrit texts into Telugu, he obtained the assistance of Acharya P. Ramachandrudu garu and Salaka Raghunatha Sarma garu. We can hardly find a parallel where a Judge contributed so much to our ancient thought and wisdom besides contributing substantially to the development of law.

2nd December, 2023.

(Justice B.P. Jeevan Reddy)

Sri K. Aravinda Rao,

Retd. Director General of Police, Andhra Pradesh

Respectful Memory of A Great Figure:

It is always a great pleasure to recall a towering personality whose memory itself infuses one with enthusiasm, courage and dedication to dharma. These were the feelings which came to my mind when I wanted to gather my memories about Just. Kodanda Ramaiah when his daughter, Smt. Parvathi, asked me to write about him. He was such a towering figure. I had the great fortune of having had association with him for about twenty years till his end. It was rather odd for an eminent retired judge to have association with a person from the police department. But this was possible because I happened to be the student of an eminent Sanskrit scholar who was highly regarded by the judge. The scholar was Padmasri Pullela SriRama Chandrudu, a scholar with nationwide repute, a person who had authored over hundred books. This common link brought me in contact with the judge also and he developed a sort of parental affection for me. I recall the times when I used to attend functions in his house along with my wife and children and almost move like members of his family.

Probably even after his retirement, Just. Kodanda Ramaiah functioned as actively as while he was handling cases as a judge in the High Court. His dedication and passion gave him indefatigable energy to work for the cause of dharma. Apart from promoting writing, he was a writer who wrote two elaborate critical appreciations, one on the Valmiki Ramayana and the other on the Mahabharata. The moral uprightness and firmness of Rama had given him a steel will and shaped his personality. The Mahabharata, the ocean of ethical and legal insights, had further sharpened his dedication for dharma. One rarely finds a person who had read every single word of the Ramayana and the Mahabharata. His attention to detail was so meticulous that he wanted to know the import of every line in the texts. It is to his credit that great philosophical works were translated into Telugu by Sri SriRamachandrudu. Arsha Vijnana Trust, a publications endeavor started by him had published all these works. This work continues even after his departure.

I recall several instances when he used to call and entrust some simple tasks such as proof-reading some Sanskrit passages, or discuss clarifications in translations and so on. Perhaps all eminent Sanskrit scholars of the state (now two states) were honoured by him. Many were associated with the translation of The Mahabharata. Thousands of students, teachers, scholars, and households have to be grateful to him for enabling them to know the grandeur of the great epics and of the philosophical works.

His attention to detail and his emphasis on clarity in communication was astonishing. It was a trait which perhaps came from his profession as a judge. He always wanted to avoid pedantic expressions but wanted simple, direct expressions in books relating to Vedanta. He was emphatic in expressing his ideas, and because of his stentorian, awe-inspiring voice one would feel as though listening to a pronouncement from the court even during a conversation.

*There is an expression in Sanskrit, pratah-smaraniya, about people whose names have to be recalled every morning as role models, and Sri Kodanda Ramaiah was one such." *****

K. Aravinda Rao

Retired D.I.Gof Police, Andhra Pradesh

Sri V. R. Reddy

Former Additional Solicitor General of India

Former Advocate General of Andhra Pradesh

At a time when the whole country is resonating with 'Ram Nam' it may not be a coincidence that Ms. Parvathi should think of scripting a biography of her illustrious father, Justice Kodandaramayya garu noted 'Ram Bhakt' who not only understood the philosophical core permeating the epic 'RAMAYANA', but also penned what he brilliantly perceived as 'LIGHT OF RAMAYANA'. Without ignoring the other epic of Hindu mythology he produced a masterpiece 'MESSAGE OF MAHABHARATHAM'.

It came as a blessing that he should get an opportunity to adorn the prestigious seat of Judge, High Court, where his duty was to in a generic sense uphold 'Dharma'. As one who had known him as a Judge and not so much as a lawyer, I can vouch for his commitment to do justice as a divine duty that rested on his shoulders. As he sat on the bench, never did he commence proceedings before a silent prayer, which did not go unnoticed. Here I recall my view expressed in a public address that the dogged faith and confidence of litigant public in the justice delivery system, despite demoralising prolixity and oppressive cost which have become its inseparable parts, presumably, springs from society's ancient belief that justice springs from a divine source.

When we think of Justice Kodandaramayya, a few significant aspects of his nature and personality come to mind. Foremost is his humility and down to earth attitude. Holding high office of Judge of High Court made no difference to his innate quality of simplicity and warm heartedness. To my knowledge he was not one who hankered for office of Judgeship. As I heard from reliable sources, when he was being considered for elevation along with Justice M. Jagannadha Rao, he had expressed his disinclination, suggesting Justice M.J. Rao be elevated as a younger person who would have better prospects for a bright future.

Yet another feature of Justice Kodandaramayya's personality was his scrupulous adherence to culture and custom of people of Telugu speaking region. No element of parochialism involved really, just a matter of valuing age old traditions. Except in court as Judge he was seen always with dhoti and angavastram. Here I'm reminded of a poem of Dr. C.Narayana Reddy highlighting tastes and habits of Telugu people.

Not too often do we come across such persons of admirable qualities of head and heart with genuine devotion to duty.

VR Reddy

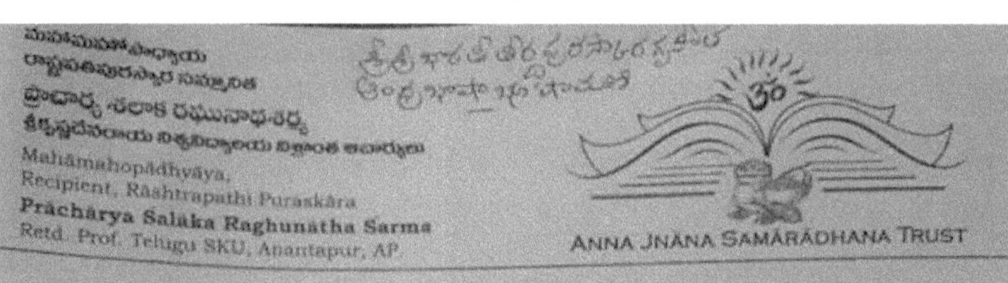

ఆదర్శప్రాయమహావ్యక్తి

శ్రీ పమిడిఘంటం కోదండరామయ్యగారు

గీతలో వాసుదేవుడు ఒక విషయాన్ని ప్రకటించారు.

ఒక మహావ్యక్తి ఒక జన్మలో యోగాన్ని అత్యంతదృఢమైన దీక్షతో ఆచరిస్తూ,

ఏదో కారణంవలన సిద్ధిదశకు చేరుకోలేకపోతే

మరుజన్మలో దానిని అందిపుచ్చుకొని సిద్ధిపర్యంతం కొనసాగిస్తాడు.

దానికోసం శుచులు, శ్రీమంతులు అయినవారి యింటిలో జన్మిస్తాడు – అని.

ఇక్కడ 'శ్రీ' అంటే ఆర్షవిద్య, సురిత్వమంటే వెనుకటిజన్మలో

జారిపోవటానికి కారణమైన కార్తిపాటి లోపాన్ని కూడా లేకుండా చేసుకోవటం.

మరొకవిధంగా చెప్పాలంటే మూడుకరణాలను

మాలిన్యం అంటకుండా చూచుకోవటం.

ఆవిధంగా యోగబలంతో ఆర్షవిద్యలో

అత్యంతసంసిద్ధిని సాధించిన మహాత్ములు యశఃకాయులు

శ్రీపమిడిఘంటం కోదండరామయ్యగారు.

వారివలన ఐహికంగా, పారమార్థికంగా జీవనంలో

పురోగతి సాధించినవారు, నావంటివారు, ఎందరో ఉన్నారు.

శ్రీవారిని ఆదర్శప్రాయవ్యక్తిగా నాహృదయంలో పదిలపరచుకొంటూ ఉంటాను.

27-11-2023   శలాక రఘునాథశర్మ

TRANSLATION

In the Bhagavadgita, Vasudeva states, "Certain great individuals, who diligently practice Yoga but face obstacles due to certain deficiencies in their spiritual discipline, are reborn into prosperous (in this context, prosperous means, in the knowledge of Arsha Vignana) and austere families.

They overcome these deficiencies by cultivating purity of thought, speech, and action (Manas, Vakku, and Karma) in their current life and transcend." Sri Kodandaramayya exemplifies one of these great personalities who have attained spiritual accomplishment. I am among those who have benefited materially and spiritually from his guidance. He will always remain in my heart as a cherished role

APARNA UPPALURI

(Granddaughter of Justice P. Kodandaramayya),

Tatagaru, my grandfather. He liked that English word very much, and he would say it out aloud, often extending the sound of the first vowel – 'What a term the Englishman has coined,' he would say. 'I am your graaaaandfather', he would say, stretching out the second syllable. For me, he embodied love and discipline. Now that I am nearly forty-five years old and a mother, I know that love is a form of discipline that is practiced unconditionally. Tatagaru planted that seed in me.

Even in his physical absence, I felt him urging me to learn, to push myself, to build my inner discipline. He always exhorted me to 'be an embodiment of purity.' As I search for the meaning of his words, they continue to echo in the hollow spaces of my bones. They became the stuff of which I'm made.

I remember his pleasure when I read to him a text that held an analysis of the Natyashastra and the prasthanatrayam (the triad of Upanishads, Brahmasutras, and Bhagavad-Gita). He ordered a copy of that book for himself, and I feel in my heart that it was the day he blessed my pursuits in the arts.

I also remember the day I excitedly told him about cell division – something I learned in biology class. It was the first time he heard about unicellular life in such detail. I was twelve; he must have been nearly sixty years old. That did not stop him from being any less excited than I was. He suddenly stopped and asked, 'Do you think amoeba has a soul?' His excitement continued unabated. 'Tell me what you learn in your biology class,' he would say, 'and I will give you an advaitin interpretation of the same idea.'

I asked him, 'How do we believe in God when we cannot see him?' He spoke to me, a curious and timid twelve-year-old child, about the difference between matter, energy, and our perceptions.

In simple words, he explained to me that if I were to gather all the energy that resides in every bit of matter in this world – that collective energy is God – 'the energy in you, the energy in me, that in the table, the chair, the tree, the star, the block of wood, the ant, and the bee – all this collectively is what we call God.' He was an advaitin – that is the explanation he gave me. It has held me together for all these years. I haven't hoped to see God, but I have hoped to experience the energy he described.

When my grandfather was performing his Sandhya, he suddenly looked up and said to me, "No one ever says, 'Lord, I want to see you.' We all pray for our difficulties to be reduced, our pain to be taken away, our wishes to be granted. But does anyone say, 'Lord, I want to see you'?" Ah! That is what I am supposed to ask for, I thought. I wonder now if that is what he asked his Lord as he sat there day after day, offering his prayers.

He left me with a desire to learn and to study, so I can make my place in this world. He left me with a yearning to live in the mystery of the Divinity he so deeply believed in.

Letters to his son studying Law in Delhi

JUSTICE P. KODANDARAMAYYA

102, Srinagar Colony,
Hyderabad - 500873
Dt: 3-9-85.

Dear Narasimha,

I am glad you informed your welfare in quick succession for which we are all happy.

I am sorry that you have not acknowledged the letter of brother which I got written to meet one senior advocate Sri P. Rameswararao. Sri Trivikramarao contacted him on phone and he promised to secure a seat in the hostel. I am particular that you should secure a seat in the hostel so that it will avoid the unnecessary disturbance for you. It might be some diversion will be there in the hostel but it is better than outside diversion and detraction.

You also meet Mr. Menon who was contacted by Mr. Veerareddy and who also promised him to secure a seat in the hostel. You must write to me what happened after you met both of them or one of them and your prospects of your getting the seat in the hostel.

I need hardly add the necessity of concentrating on studies. Yesterday I received a call from the Dean of the Osmania University stating that he reserved a seat for you as they felt very unhappy last year that they could not secure a seat. But to my dismay and to their dismay I told them that my son had already left for Delhi and he joined the Law College at that place. You must justify your decision though it is a bit inconvenience to the members of the family. I shall be happy either if you secure your seat in I.A.S. or equip yourself to practice in Supreme Court. But in the latter case there will be a lot of waiting period which I will not mind if you do really concentrate on the profession. You must keep your health trim either by running or playing regularly games. Check your habit of irregular sleeping. Fortunately all these years I am not having any problem with my children as they are always with me. Though you have sufficiently grown up mother is not quite reconcilable for your absence but she is very rosy in her dreams that you will secure for her a pride in-deed by securing I.A.S. rank. I am not anxious about that job but I am very particular that you should equip yourself well for any walk of life and this is the cream of your educational career which you must reach its

Letters to his son studying Law in Delhi

:2:

pinnacle There is a delay in sending Draft. I shall send as you desire to in the name of State Bank of India tomorrow. and you open an account in the nearby bank. I wish you should not be in a hurry to secure a room as you have to pay advance and other things. If your efforts to secure a seat in the hostel are not fruitful then you can think of securing the room. I am posting this letter to avoid further delay. Tomorrow I shall send the Draft. I wish that you should inform in advance Sri Ramakrishna rao that you would come and participate in the Pooja of Vinayakachavithi on 18-9-85. You read regularly the 12th Chapter. If you do not have the book you purchase one.

The address of Sri P.P. Rao is as follows:-

Sri P. Parameswararao,
Senior Advocate,
34/22 East Patel Nagar
Phone No.587624

Brother Raghu wrote this address to your first address given to us. Perhaps you have not received it. Please contact both Sri P.P. Rao and also Menon and make every effort to secure a seat in the hostel.

Yours affectionately,

(P. KODANDARAMAYYA)

Mr.P.S.V.L.Narasimha,
C/o V. Seshadayee,
Block 12, Q. 463
Sector-I
Haig Square
Goll Market
New Delhi 110001.

Letters to his son studying Law in Delhi

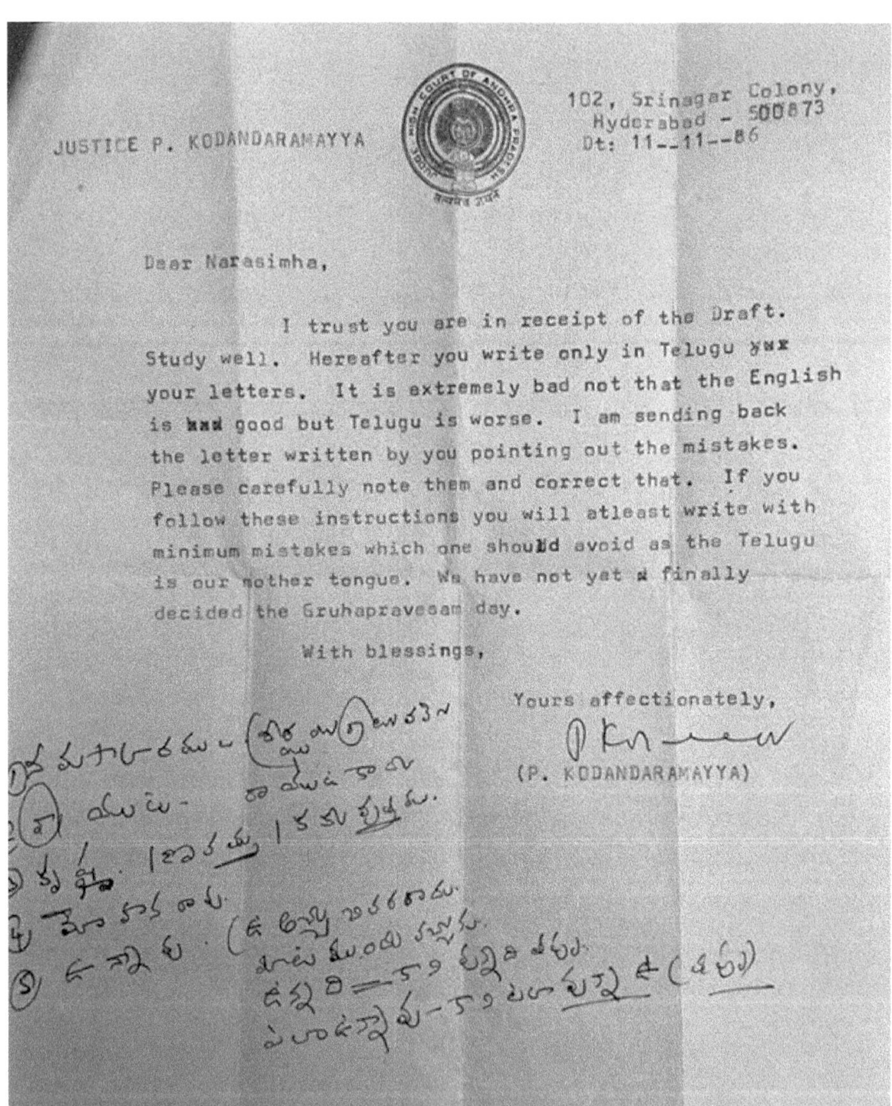

JUSTICE P. KODANDARAMAYYA

102, Srinagar Colony,
Hyderabad - 500873
Dt: 11--11--86

Dear Narasimha,

I trust you are in receipt of the Draft. Study well. Hereafter you write only in Telugu your letters. It is extremely bad not that the English is good but Telugu is worse. I am sending back the letter written by you pointing out the mistakes. Please carefully note them and correct that. If you follow these instructions you will atleast write with minimum mistakes which one should avoid as the Telugu is our mother tongue. We have not yet finally decided the Gruhapravesam day.

With blessings,

Yours affectionately,

(P. KODANDARAMAYYA)

Letters to his son studying Law in Delhi

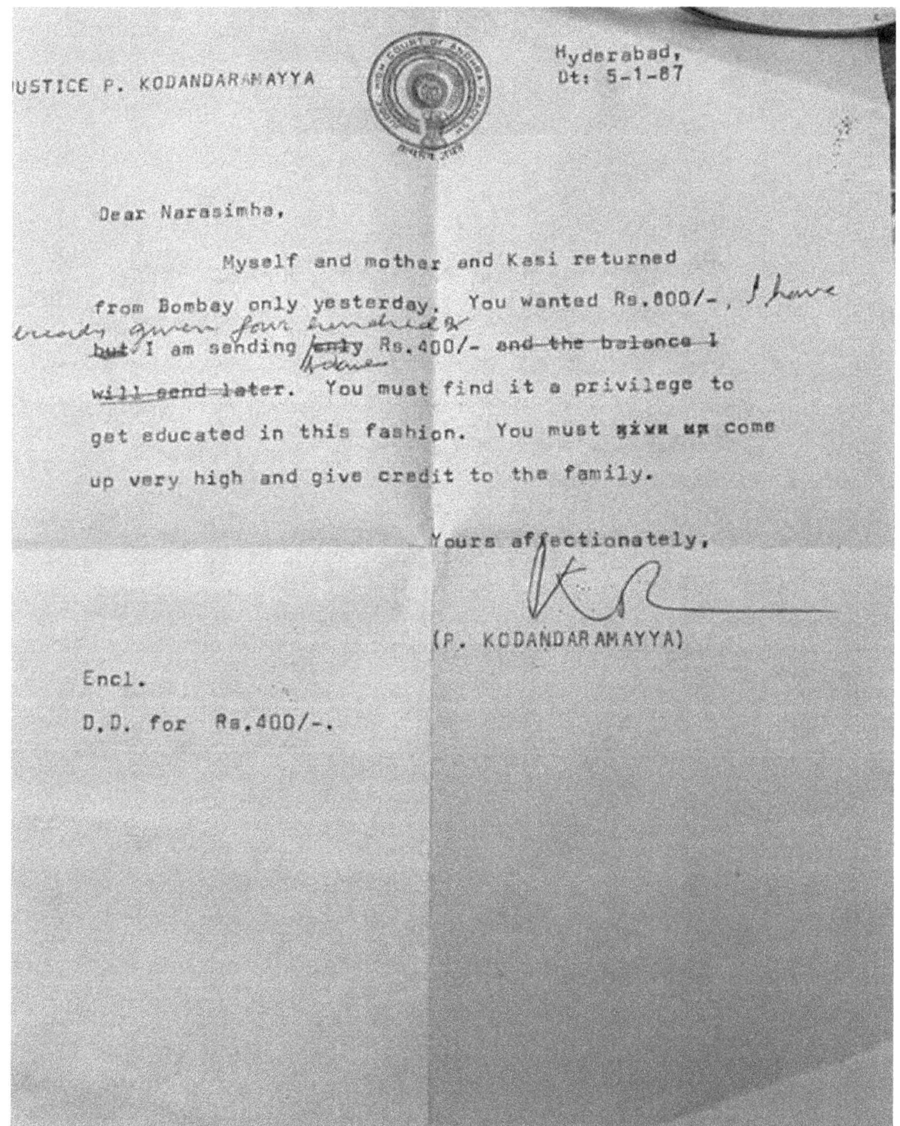

JUSTICE P. KODANDARAMAYYA

Hyderabad,
Dt: 5-1-87

Dear Narasimha,

Myself and mother and Kasi returned from Bombay only yesterday. You wanted Rs.600/-, I have already given four hundred & but I am sending only Rs.400/- and the balance I will send later. You must find it a privilege to get educated in this fashion. You must come up very high and give credit to the family.

Yours affectionately,

(P. KODANDARAMAYYA)

Encl.

D.D. for Rs.400/-.

Justice Sanjay Kumar
Judge, Supreme Court of India

Bungalow No. 6,
Motilal Nehru Marg,
New Delhi-110011
Tel. : 011-23013454
011-23011361

MESSAGE

My association with late Sri Justice Kodandaramayya Garu dates back to my college days. His son, Narasimha, was not only a classmate but also my roommate while we were doing our LLB at Delhi and I would frequently visit their home at Hyderabad during the holidays. Despite his busy schedule as a sitting Judge of the AP High Court, he always took time to guide and encourage us. As an Advocate, I appeared before him a few times and I remember attending his farewell in Court No. 7. In those days, the practice of having a Full Court farewell was not there and the farewell speech of the retiring Judge was delivered in his own Court after the address of the Advocate General. Court Hall No. 7 is not very big, but it was packed to the gills for the occasion – in recognition of how highly he was regarded by members of the Bar.

Though, Justice Kodandaramayya Garu was a Judge for just six years, he left an indelible mark in the annals of the institution. I may point out one instance when, as a member of a Full Bench, in *Maddineni Kondaiah vs. Yaseen Fatima and others* (AIR 1986 AP 62), Justice Kodandaramayya Garu authored a separate opinion. The issue was whether the insurance of a vehicle would lapse upon the transfer thereof without a certificate of registration. Justice Kodandaramayya Garu agreed with the lead opinion that the policy would not lapse. The Supreme Court had occasion to deal with this very issue in *G. Govindan vs. New India Assurance Co. Ltd.* [(1999) 3 SCC 754]. The Court considered whether the AP High Court's view in *Maddineni Kondaiah* was correct or the Delhi and Karnataka High Courts' Full Bench judgments to the contrary were correct. The Supreme Court concurred with the view taken by the AP High Court and, in that context, the opinion authored by Justice Kodandaramayya Garu was quoted copiously and at great length by the Supreme Court!

Justice Kodandaramayya Garu was deeply religious and spiritual. His treatises on the Ramayana and the Mahabharata take one beyond the narrative of those great epics to present the right way of living one's life. I am truly delighted that Parvati Garu, his elder daughter, took up the task of writing his biography. I find that her easy style of narrating his life story reads more like an entertaining parable but, at the same time, beautifully conveys his principled and righteous way of life. Justice Kodandaramayya Garu was and will always remain a great source of inspiration and guidance to those who believe in an order of living, ordained by ethics and higher values.

Sanjay Kumar
(Justice Sanjay Kumar)

A.K JAYAPRAKASH RAO

ADVOCATE
STANDING COUNSEL
TIRUMALA TIRUPATHI DEVASTHANAMS

Mobile : 9246582225

Off : 3-4-206/2, Lingampally,
Hyderabad - 500 027.
E-mail : akjayaprakashrao@gmail.com

Date.............................

Dated : 16-12-2023

My memories with Late Respectable Late Sri Justice Kodandaramayya Garu started when I was introduced by my late Senior Sri. M.V. Bharati, Advocate in the year 1973.

Ever since, my introduction, I was frequently meeting him in High Court and used to discuss various legal issues in Labour and service matters and he used to give guidance to me for conducting and arguing the cases. During the period from 1973 onwards he has developed love and affection towards me by encouraging me he moulded my life and gave several advices to withstand in this competitive and noble profession.

He was always showing compassion towards the litigant of weaker section and helping them as much as possible whenever I have entrusted the matters to him.

His association changed the way of my life and made me to lead spiritual and devotional life and he used to take me holy places whenever he has visiting Badrachalem, Ghanghapur and Mantralayam and invariably I used to accompany him.

My association with him was is immemorial in my life and I am so much indebted to him in changing my way of life.

With kind regards,

AK Jayaprakash Rao,
Advocate
High Court of State Telangana

265

Lived life to the fullest

About the Author

Parvathi Uppaluri's journey is quite remarkable and diverse. Returning to India after a significant period abroad, she has chosen to immerse herself in rural life near Bangalore, dedicating her efforts to the upliftment of underprivileged children and women. Her establishment of a school for the children of daily wage and small-time farmers reflects her commitment to providing education and opportunities where they are needed most.

Having lived in Algeria and Canada, Parvathi brings a wealth of multicultural experience to her work. Her background as a counsellor and life skills coach has equipped her with the tools to support a wide range of individuals, from marginalized women on social assistance to youth and new immigrants in Canada. By helping them navigate employment opportunities and integrate into society, she has played a vital role in their empowerment and self-discovery.

Her literary pursuits further showcase her talents and passion. Writing eight short stories in her mother tongue, Telugu, as well as penning her father's biography in the same language, she not only preserves her cultural heritage but also shares her experiences and wisdom with a broader audience. The publication of her works adds another dimension to her contributions, allowing her to inspire and connect with even more people.

Parvathi Uppaluri's story is one of resilience, compassion, and dedication to making a difference in the lives of others, regardless of geographical boundaries or cultural differences. Her work serves as an inspiration for aspiring change makers and underscores the power of individual action in creating positive social change.